Shaving Lessons

Iris:

Your words for the jacket are sheer poetry — marvelously vivid and very very generous. I can only hope I live up to your Billy Crystal comparison should I one day break into stand-up comedy! My sincere gratitude for your help!

June 2000

Shaving Lessons

A MEMOIR OF FATHER AND SON

Kurt Chandler

CHRONICLE BOOKS

SAN FRANCISCO

Library of Congress Cataloging-in-Publication Data:
Chandler, Kurt.
    Shaving lessons : a memoir of father and son / Kurt Chandler.
        p.   cm.
    ISBN 0-8118-2360-1
1. Chandler, Kurt. 2. Chandler, Benjamin—Childhood and youth.
3. Fathers and sons—Wisconsin—Milwaukee Region—Biography.
4. Milwaukee Region (Wis.)—Biography. I. Title.

CT275.C458 A3 2000
977.5'94033'0922—dc21
[B]   99-087657

Printed in the United States of America

Book design by Blue Design
Cover photos: Digital Imagery ® copyright © 1999 by Photodisc, Inc.
Typeset in Franklin Gothic, Janson, and Grotesque Six.

Distributed in Canada by
Raincoast Books
8680 Cambie Street
Vancouver, British Columbia V6P 6M9

10 9 8 7 6 5 4 3 2 1

Chronicle Books
85 Second Street
San Francisco, California 94105

www.chroniclebooks.com

For my father and my son

CONTENTS

Hero

Benjamin is a high school freshman. The years are counting down, the frames are flashing by. One morning, and it won't be long, he will push his chair back from the kitchen table, thank his mother for the pancakes, kiss his sister on the forehead, pat me on my bald spot, pick up his duffel bag, and walk out the door forever to make his way in the world, no longer a resident member of his biological family. At that moment, I will have reached that rueful time when I will be without his smiling face in my everyday life. Out of the picture will go my hero.

I used to have other heroes: pop idols, mainly, athletes and movie stars, musicians and writers, even a politician or two— James Dean and Mickey Mantle, Gene McCarthy and Kurt Vonnegut. Paul McCartney was a hero once. It wasn't the mop-top haircut that captured my envy, it was his voice; I wanted his voice, those high notes that he could belt out at the end of "Hey Jude."

But today, my hero is my teenage son. As he grows up, I'm trading roles with him and he's becoming my hope, proxy of my ambitious life quests, striving for all I have strived for and much more. As he shoots as tall as me, he's becoming a sensible and sharp-witted young adult, much more sensible and sharp-witted than I was at age fourteen. It's gratifying to see him outsmart me, outrun me, outdo me, succeeding where I fell short at his age, attempting things I never would have tried. That's all a father can hope for, a child who will pull himself up a rung or two on the evolutionary ladder.

Let me tell you a few things about Ben: He's got one green eye and one brown, caps on two front teeth from an encounter long ago with a backyard swing, a small scar on his nose from an encounter long ago with a wood-burning stove. He can name the capitals of all fifty states and has traveled to thirty-six. He can't carry a tune (no Paul McCartney in this boy), but he can play a near-perfect rendition of "The Dance of the Marionettes" on the piano. He's an awful speller, but has a rich vocabulary and uses words like "personify" and "grandiose" in school term papers and even in conversation, though once in a while he'll trip himself up by saying something like "The operating word here is . . ." when he really means "The *operative* word."

Ben is hard to pigeonhole; he blurs many lines. He's a jock and a nerd, a second baseman on the high school baseball team and a member of the debate team. He's a math whiz and a wordsmith, the youngest in his precalculus class and the youngest on the staff of the student newspaper. The first CD he bought was by the Crash Test Dummies, but he's been imitating Bob Dylan's nasal whine for years. His T-shirts tend to be white or black. He owns just a single necktie (which I've borrowed several times). He has videotaped all but six episodes of "The Simpsons" and counts *To Kill a Mockingbird* as one of his favorite novels. At the breakfast table, against my protests (*always* against my protests), he uses the morning comics as a placemat and dribbles peanut butter from his cinnamon toast onto the forlorn face of Charlie Brown.

Ben is caught in that peculiar place called adolescence, leaping, plunging, tumbling head over heels in the surging current toward the shoals of adulthood. He still allows his father to hug him occasionally, but wouldn't be caught dead in a pair of deck shoes, chinos, and a polo shirt, my regular attire. It's an awkward place, adolescence, a place somewhere between sheer bliss and total humiliation: One summer day, on the Atlantic coast, the two of us were walking along the beach. As I gazed at the ocean, Ben amused himself by digging his feet deep into the sand and walking backwards, studying his own footprints—completely oblivious to two young women who were sunbathing topless nearby.

That's an endearing image to me, and a good metaphor for Ben as a teenager—trudging toward manhood even as he steps backwards, head down, laughing to himself.

I, meanwhile, am trudging along on another route. With my eye on the horizon, I'm slouching ever so reluctantly toward middle age, trying to stoke a freewheelin' spirit that was sparked when I was my son's age while grudgingly giving in to loose-fit jeans and reading glasses.

To tell you a few things about myself: I've worked as a busboy, taxi driver, shipping clerk, construction worker, printing press operator, fence builder, handyman, folk singer, youth advocate, newspaper reporter, freelance writer, writing coach, magazine editor, and author. I went to catechism at St. Mary's Catholic Church every Saturday morning from ages six to fourteen, with a growing reluctance. I didn't learn how to swim until I was thirteen, didn't graduate from college until I was twenty-eight, and didn't realize the benefits of physical fitness until I was thirty-nine. Some of my best friends are guys I've known since high school. Like many men in their forties, I'm tired of yard work and I worry about my prostate. I too can name the capitals of all fifty states (with a little help from Ben). I'm good at starting a campfire. I admit to liking bagpipes. I regret never having learned any formal dance steps. I'm a full inch taller than the official height printed on my driver's license (five feet, *ten* inches). When out for dinner with friends, I'm usually the one who orders the disappointing entree. To my son's utter embarrassment, I still wear shirts that I bought before he was born. Among my most cherished possessions are my father's pocket watch, a black-and-white photograph of my mother and me taken days after I was born, a chunk of rose quartz given to me by my wife, my Martin D-18 guitar, a worn but complete collection of John Steinbeck's novels, and an IMPEACH NIXON bumper sticker that I peeled from my 1970 Volkswagen Beetle before it was towed away to the junkyard. The biggest thrills of my life have been (in no particular order) climbing to the summit of Longs Peak (elevation: 14,255 feet) in Colorado, flying in a helicopter over Death Valley (280 feet below sea level), having my picture taken as a boy with Hank Aaron, smoking a joint with Allen Ginsberg in college, and witnessing the births of my two children.

Ben and I belong to a family of four. His mother, Cathy, and I were married when we were both twenty-four. It was the first marriage for each of us and, with periodic tune-ups, it's still running strong. Ben's sister, Emma, born nearly nine years later than Ben, started kindergarten on the same day he entered high school, a big day for the lot of us.

Ben and I are first-born Chandler males, as was my father. Born June 4, 1930, Kent Chandler was the first of two sons, a child of the Depression years, raised in Milwaukee by his mother after his father died when he was just a boy. I was the first of four siblings, three boys and one girl, a Milwaukee native born into the guileless fifties. Ben (the name *Benjamin* in Hebrew means "first son") also was the first Chandler of his generation, born in Colorado during the fickle eighties.

My father was a carpenter. Probably more than anything else, he enjoyed crafting things out of wood. His trade was his livelihood, his passion, his sanctuary, his honor. A slender man of medium height, he was always in movement, always in the middle of a project. When I was eight or nine, he built a wooden footbridge to span a creek that ran along the boundary of our suburban backyard. He worked on that bridge for a month or more, spending evenings and weekends sawing the pine boards to size, sanding and planing the planks to perfection. I would stand and watch him in the garage, transfixed by the shriek of the power saw, breathing in the sweet smell of fresh sawdust. Sometimes he asked me to help, instructing me to hold a board steady as he sawed off the end. The bridge was massive (as I remember it), maybe eight feet high, four feet wide, and ten feet long. Its design was quite elaborate: high, curved railings on each side to prevent anyone from tumbling into the water, an arched wooden canopy to provide shelter from the rain and add a touch of elegance.

When it was completed, my father painted the bridge white, top to bottom, and on a Sunday morning, while all of the neighbors were at church, he hoisted it into the back of his Dodge van, transported it from the garage to the backyard, and positioned it over the creek that separated our yard from the yards of the families beyond. It was a magnanimous gesture, symbolic and yet practical, a gift of pure neighborliness.

I remember watching him years later as he led my son across that bridge when Ben was barely old enough to walk—the proud grandfather on his way to the neighbors to show off his first grandchild. The bridge was worn to bare wood, in need of a fresh coat of paint. But it was still standing.

My father only made it to age fifty-eight. He died of cancer when Ben was six. It has been up to me to acquaint Ben with a grandfather he barely knew.

My memories of my father are bittersweet. I remember many golden moments together—throwing a baseball around the backyard, settling into a studied silence over a chessboard. But as I entered my teenage years, the darker days began to overshadow the bright. As is the case with too many fathers and teenage sons of an earlier generation, we never took the time to get to know each other well enough to grasp our disagreements, to understand our differences or our similarities. My father and mother were not rich or well educated, but they worked hard at taking care of their four children, striving to give us every advantage they could, guiding us along. As I reached adolescence, though, their guidance seemed to turn to exhortation. They taught me how to behave but not how to live. They taught me the rules but not the reasons.

15

Adolescence became a closed door, and I began to feel out of place in what seemed more and more like *their* home and less and less like mine.

I don't subscribe to the belief that adolescence must be a polarizing time for parents and teens. To the contrary, it has become a fundamental duty of men of my generation to build a better relationship with our sons and daughters than we had with our fathers. Today's dads work hard at laying the foundation of a true kinship between their children and themselves. I see Ben's first year in high school as a cornerstone of that foundation.

I do not want to mold him into a younger me. It can't be done. And I do not want to be his best friend. Rather, I want to define fatherhood as a relationship rather than just a role. I will understand my son as a person—his interests and tastes, his anger and humor, his *essence*. I hope he will know me as both a father and as a man. And from this understanding, I hope a mutual respect will result, and an enduring bond.

This book is about forging that bond with my son, and about a deeper understanding of my own adolescence and my own father, who was, it is easier to see now, both a father and a man. This book is about Ben in the first and pivotal year of high school, and about me, in my own pivotal—and dual—role.

Ben began high school with a dizzying trepidation. Gone were the recesses, spelling bees, and innocent chaperoned dances of middle school. In their places were driver's ed, bad skin, and classmates with breasts or beards. "There's so much to think about," he said after his first couple of days in the ninth grade. "It's like total chaos, but exciting, too."

As Ben came face to face with that psycho-socio-physical condition known as high school, I too found myself facing a mass of changes. In some ways, our life changes arrived in tandem. I moved my family from Minneapolis back to my hometown after leaving twenty years earlier—a baby boomer returning to his roots. Cathy and I sold our home in Minnesota, rented a house outside of Milwaukee, and started over. In the process, I made a long-anticipated shift in my career, quitting a job as a newspaper reporter and replacing it with the unfettered though precarious life of a freelance writer and part-time teacher. Cathy, meanwhile, switched directions as well, enrolling again in college, full time.

It has been an eventful year, especially for Ben and me, embarking on journeys through parallel universes—adolescence and middle age. For me, our parallel passages have been instructive and stabilizing. A teenager, despite all the turmoil, can bring a sense of purpose into a home. Ben's the-world-is-my-oyster highs have served as an antidote to my woe-is-me midlife blues. There is little time for me to get bogged down in angst and self-doubt; too much is going on. In his headlong dash into adolescence, Ben unknowingly has helped me reconcile my own changes. While I've been helping him shape his values, he has helped me restore mine, reminding me of what is important, and what is not.

School Days

The newspaper hits the front porch with a *thunk* and I'm jarred awake, eyes wide. The sounds of morning drift through the open window: the nagging caw of a crow, the jangle of a dog collar, the steady clap of running shoes on pavement. The air is warm, the sun is up. But this Monday is a little different from the last. Labor Day is still a week away, yet there's a sign of autumn in the air, marked not by falling leaves or dipping temperatures but by the rushing expectancy that comes with the beginning of a school year.

Summer is officially over. We're back on the clock.

I shuffle down the stairs to the kitchen and switch on the electric coffee maker.

"Good morning, Benny," I sing out. Ben turns his head in my direction, almost makes eye contact, and gives an incomprehensible grunt in return. He has been up for an hour, showered, and dressed in clothes he picked out with great deliberation the night before, with more deliberation than is evident in his current appearance: He wears a pair of baggy blue-jean shorts, a blue T-shirt with LATE NIGHT WITH DAVID LETTERMAN stamped in bright yellow across the chest, white athletic socks purposely bunched up at his ankles, and black high-top Converse sneakers tied in double knots—pretty much the same uniform he's worn all summer. His hair is combed, parted in the middle, and carefully laid over his ever-so-slightly protruding ears. His teeth are brushed and sparkling, a gap between his two front teeth visible if and when he smiles.

Ben is stepping into high school today, a freshman in the class of 2000.

He sits hunched at the breakfast table, elbows on the tabletop, chin in his hands, a half-eaten waffle on a plate to his right, and the morning paper spread out in front of him. He taps his foot to the tick of the wall clock as he scans the comics. But his eyes wander, they dart around the room, following my movement from the cupboard to the refrigerator to the coffeepot. He breaks off another bite of the waffle with his fork, takes a big swallow of orange juice, and, with a trace of alarm in his voice, blurts out: "*Look.*" His finger points to a pimple about the size of a cantaloupe at the end of his nose.

I shrink my face into a squint and edge closer. "I can hardly see it," I lie, trying to douse his panic and save him from vanity. "Don't sweat it."

But his mother knows better. She can recognize a crisis in the making a mile away. Tired but alert, Cathy appears in the doorway in her long chenille bathrobe, ready to the rescue.

She looks at Ben's face. "Come into the bathroom for a minute," she says, and he follows, suspicious but desperate. She digs around in the medicine chest and from a shelf takes a small bottle of makeup. She shakes the bottle, opens the top, and measures a drop onto the tip of her finger. Ben looks at her, appalled, but willing to go along with it. With the failings of Clearasil and Oxy Pads, it's time for extreme measures. He leans forward. Cathy applies the drop to his nose, carefully dabs and models the makeup, and the zit disappears.

"No one will ever know," Cathy says softly, screwing the bottle top back on. "But you might want to slip this into your pocket."

"You think I'm gonna put on makeup at school? No way, Mom." He looks into the bathroom mirror, approvingly. His bright red nose has been dulled to the color of putty.

Ben claps his hands together and walks into the dining room, taking long, purposeful strides across the wooden floor. He's practicing a new walk. Now that he's in high school, he figures, he'll need to change his gait to make an impression. He'll be one of the many unproven, an unknown. He'll want to show his peers and his teachers that he has confidence, control, aplomb. He can't be squirrelly and gawky anymore, swinging his arms out at his side every which way and tripping over his own two feet like he did in middle school. A high school walk must be fresh, must be fluid, limbs in sync, head back, a movement that says I am here, I have arrived, I'm all that *is*.

Ben stalks into the living room, his weight on his heels, his knees bending deep with each step, his shoulders slightly bowed, his chin out. He turns back to the dining room, then back again to the living room.

"I can't see Big Bird," protests his sister. Emma is lying on the sofa in her pajamas. Ben's new walk is blocking her view of "Sesame Street" on the TV screen.

"Well hey there, little Emma," Ben says and gives her a kiss on the forehead. "Ready for your big day?"

It's an important day for Emma as well. Today she starts kindergarten.

"What will I get to eat at my school?" Emma asks.

"You'll probably get a snack," he says. "You'll go outside and play on the swings and make all kinds of new friends. You'll have a great time."

Emma is dubious, but she'll take her brother's word for it, if anybody's.

Ben circles the dining-room table and unzips his backpack, checking the contents one more time. Plain black canvas pack, nothing stylish, no logos or swoosh marks, bought at an Army surplus store after weeks of searching, the backpack will be his life-support system for the next nine months. Today it's only half full, holding blank spiral notebooks, empty folders, a graphing calculator, and a bag lunch—a peanut-butter-and-jelly sandwich, apple, and potato chips, prepared by Ben's own hands. By the end of the week, the backpack will be bulging with homework assignments and textbooks as heavy as bricks.

I try to ease his anxiousness. "You know, Ben, when I was your age . . .," I say, playfully, but he won't be humored. High school is no laughing matter. The pimple on his nose is just one of his many worries. He worries that someone will call him "Shorty." He worries that someone else will make fun of his big ears. And he worries that yet another tormentor will give him a "bubbler ride," which he has described as an upperclassman sneaking up from behind, lifting an unsuspecting freshman from under the arms, sitting him down into a drinking fountain, and turning on the water.

Ben walks to the bathroom for a final inspection. Emma follows close behind, climbs onto the rim of the bathtub next to the sink, and looks into the mirror. She opens her mouth, grasps a tooth between two fingers, and yanks furiously. It's her first loose tooth, and she wants the booty.

"How much money does the Tooth Fairy give?" she quizzes Ben for the hundred-fiftieth time.

"I think you'll get about twenty dollars," Ben says, tired of the question, and she yanks a little harder, grimacing into the mirror.

I hear their conversation from the kitchen.

"No, no, that's not exactly . . .," I try to explain. "See, the Tooth Fairy doesn't have a whole lot of money, Emma. She gives children, oh, maybe a dollar for each tooth."

That's still enough incentive for her to keep yanking.

Emma is dressed in a white Pocahontas T-shirt, pink shorts, and white ankle socks. Her long, dark hair is pulled back into a French braid. Her bright brown eyes signal high enthusiasm. Ben stands at her side in the bathroom, and as I watch them ponder their reflections in the glass it's clearer than ever that they are of separate generations.

21

Ben and Emma are nine years apart and have no middle sibling to bridge the gulf. Every family decision seems to turn into a controversy because of the discrepancy in their ages. Do we get Chinese takeout or a Happy Meal? Do we watch a feature-length cartoon or PG-13? Almost nightly, the chronological separation makes for a discombobulating discussion at the dinner table. One minute Ben is sharing his understanding of "parabolas" and "quartic equations," and the next Emma is trying to one-up him with boasts of her latest feat on the monkey bars. Now that Emma can load the VCR and Ben has his own collection of CDs, it's not unusual to get caught in the crossfire of Disney and Smashing Pumpkins.

But I've come to see this age separation as a good thing. Ben and Emma hang out together. They get along. Their affection for each other pulls each of them toward a middle ground, though Ben is pulled a bit harder sometimes by his stubborn little sister. She's half his size, yet they have things in common. Ben patiently accompanies his sister as she pedals her tricycle around the block. And Emma sits elbow-to-elbow with her brother as he shows her the intricacies of the latest computer game.

On the good days, the two bring out the best in each other. Emma learns courage, determination, and self-confidence through Ben's example. Lately, even Ben's teenage political correctness is beginning to rub off. Emma listens intently as he admonishes her for watching the classic animated *Peter Pan* video, explaining how the depiction of Indians as dangerous savages is distorted and insulting. Likewise, though unknowingly, Emma makes her own mark on Ben. He learns patience by caring for her, playing with her, teaching her how to float on her back in the neighborhood wading pool and how to read traffic signs in the car. Through his sister's wide-eyed innocence ("How do they make cartoons?"), Ben remains playful and curious, allowing himself to hold onto his own childhood just a bit longer without feeling too sappy about it.

"I've got to go now, Emma," Ben says as he lifts her from the edge of the tub, putting her on the floor.

"But school doesn't start for another forty-five minutes," says his mother, leading Emma into the kitchen for breakfast.

"Yeah, but I've got to meet Pete and Dan. We're going to walk together."

There's strength in numbers, and Ben is glad to have won the friendships over the summer of Pete and Dan, two boys he met in middle school. Pete and Dan are neighbors; they've known each other for years. Dan has an older brother in high school and knows the school. But it is Ben who is the leader of his pack today. He's the boy most familiar with the school. When he topped out in math last year in eighth grade, he began reporting to the high school once a week for tutoring in trigonometry. He knows the lay of the land at Wauwatosa East High School, and his buddies look to him now for a little leadership.

"I'm glad I'm done with middle school," he suddenly confides as he swings his backpack over his shoulders. "High school will be much better. I get along a lot better with older kids."

"You've always gotten along better with people older than you," I tell him. "When we were living in Colorado, your mother and I had very few friends with kids. So when you were born, you were surrounded by adults. We used to have Thanksgiving dinners at our house every year. We'd add a couple of leaves to the dining room table and plunk you down in your high chair. I can still see you, you were maybe a year old, squeezing your mashed potatoes through your fingers like it was Play Doh. You were the house prince. And good comic relief."

"Whatever," Ben says. "I'm just glad to get out of Longfellow. High school's got to be more interesting."

Longfellow Middle School was, in Ben's words, "as typical a middle school as you can get"—a traditional color-within-the-lines school, with classes that were seldom stimulating and teachers who had run out of ideas. His year at Longfellow was limiting, unchallenging. Though he'll be a lowly freshman, he has been looking forward to meeting new kids, different kids, and to teachers that might stretch his imagination.

Cathy and I escort him to the front door. He pauses, brushes his hair back, places a blue baseball cap carefully on his head, and adjusts the visor. Then he opens the glass door and steps onto the planked porch. Ben's time has come.

"Just be yourself today," says Cathy, and she throws her arms around his shoulders. She releases her hold and he nods, then tromps down the steps, his weight on his heels, his back bowed, his chin pointed straight ahead.

"And try to keep a lid on the attitude," I chime in from the open door. He moves down the sidewalk and across the street, and I call out, though not too loudly, "We love you, son."

Ben crosses the street and briskly sidesteps a threesome of middle schoolers walking in the same direction. He will cut a new route this morning. Down the hill, in the shade of towering oaks and maples, he will turn left at the blue mailbox instead of right and weave through the neighborhood to the high school. Along the way, he will hook up with Pete and Dan, and they will take their own sweet time walking the remaining blocks, joking and laughing, moving in a clump of three, elbowing each other down the sidewalk, working off their nervous energy so early in the day.

Wauwatosa East High School, known as Tosa East, is a school of about thirteen hundred students. It is an older school, brown brick, three stories. The top floor was sealed off and abandoned years ago when asbestos began flaking from the ceiling and school officials decided it was too costly to remove. For generations, East has been a reliable feeder school to the University of Wisconsin, sending some of its brightest to Madison, an hour away. Tosa East is at the very center of Wauwatosa (Ojibwa for "fireflies"), a first-ring suburb just west of Milwaukee. The school is only a few blocks from the channeled banks of the Menimonee River, which runs through the town's historical village—a French bakery, an

Italian restaurant, a cyber cafe, an ice-cream parlor, a bookstore, a hardware store, a bank, and a tavern or two.

Day and night, the high school seems to be bustling with activities. Except for the occasional pot busts and the time authorities found what they thought (mistakenly) were the components of a bomb in a student's locker, the activities are wholesome.

For the first day of the school year, a stream of red and white banners have been stretched across the lobby like banners at the starting line of a marathon. The tile floors of the hallways—so much wider than the halls in middle school—have been polished and for the moment are unscuffed. The principal stands outside the school office greeting students, recalling names from last year and memorizing new ones. And teachers wait at their classroom doors, ready to begin.

The students will take their seats in the fluorescent glare in the math rooms and science labs and English classes. A bell will jolt them into attentiveness, and their names will be called from a roster. Their books will open and their minds will follow, new sensibilities of the world will form, and there will be no looking back.

Just four blocks away, but in a different galaxy, is Washington Elementary School. Emma skips along the sidewalk between Cathy and me, each of her small hands in one of ours, her new Tweety Bird backpack strapped to her small body. As we arrive at the schoolyard, her confidence collapses. The yard is a sea of pink-faced children and parents, all strangers to Emma. Kids crowd the playground, swarming on the slides and swings and jungle gym. In the midst of this chaos, teachers hold up small signs bearing their names and classroom numbers, like chauffeurs awaiting arrivals in an airport concourse.

"There she is," says Cathy, pointing to Emma's teacher, and we file in line behind the other families. I am heartened to see that a good share of the parents are fathers, some in jeans and polo shirts, some in business suits and ties, interrupting their 8-to-5 routines for the send-off. This will be my joyful routine, delivering Emma to kindergarten each morning.

The bell rings and we follow Emma's teacher into the classroom. Emma holds her best friend, Buttons the Cat, a black-and-white stuffed animal, to her chest and wraps her other arm around her mother's leg. Her lower lip quivers and huge tears well in her eyes as Cathy tries to extricate herself from her grasp and seat her with the rest of the children on a rug in front of the teacher's storytelling chair.

The teacher mercifully intervenes, sweeping Emma onto her lap as she begins reading a story, a story about another cat. Cathy and I walk backward out of the classroom, waving reassuringly as we go.

Cathy is the last to set out from home this morning. After returning from Emma's school, she hastily gathers her own school supplies. Cathy began classes herself a day earlier, working toward a degree in education at a women's college in Milwaukee. She's fueled by the same nervous enthusiasm exhibited by her freshman son and kindergarten daughter.

"See you later," she says, book bag slung over one shoulder, purse over the other, coffee cup in one hand, car keys in the other. "I'll pick up Emma on my way home from school. Have a good day." She blows me a kiss and slams the door behind her.

The house is silent. I'm home alone with the clock and the calendar. I'm tempted to turn on the television and waste away an hour or so, but guilt tugs at my shoulders. I follow my conscience down a flight of stairs and into my basement office, feeling orphaned from the outside world and more than a little envious of Cathy and the kids.

I switch on the computer and settle into my desk chair. I am comfortable in my basement bunker, surrounded by books and Emma's homemade artwork and shelves filled with toys the kids have outgrown. The windows are covered with heavy curtains to seal out diversion, and a space heater blows warm air at my feet, its steady orange glow like the embers of a campfire. But as the computer groans to service, I can't concentrate. Distraction comes easily. I check my email. I tune the radio to a talk show. I leaf through the pages of a magazine and fiddle with odds and ends on my desktop—a paperweight, a chunk of bottle glass found on the shore of some lake, a Magic 8 Ball.

Every day is judgment day as a freelance writer, I grumble to myself. A few months ago, the future looked a lot brighter from this chair. I had quit a job at a Minneapolis newspaper, nearing burnout, and was happily returning home to Milwaukee. Like other middle-aging baby boomers, I had a longing to be closer to family and friends. My widowed mother could use the help of her oldest son, I reasoned, and Ben and Emma would grow closer to their aunts and uncles and cousins. I was ready to look homeward.

Cathy agreed to make the leap. She enrolled Ben in eighth grade in Wauwatosa while I tied up loose ends in Minnesota. I made the final drive alone. I filled my sky blue 1983 Subaru wagon with the last of our possessions: houseplants, record albums, clothes, my old acoustic guitar. Topping the load were paintings and sculptures that we had collected over the years, some of them valuable. In my satchel on the passenger's seat was our life savings. Rolling down the interstate on a crisp morning, hauling a booty of checks and artwork in a rusty rat trap of a car— 142,000 miles on the odometer, brakes functional on just three of four wheels, an ignition that turned only with a screwdriver—I couldn't have felt more liberated. Music played loudly on the tape deck, something fabulously portentous, Dylan's "Like a Rolling Stone." The eastern sun shone on my face, and I was heading home to start anew, healthy and free of debt, unsure of what would come next but untroubled by the uncertainty.

It felt like a freedom I'd known decades earlier, before our children were born, before I was married. I had been traveling by motorcycle with my friend Michael. We'd been on the road for two solid months. Each day was unplanned, spontaneous. On one particular afternoon, we traveled through Glacier National Park on our way into the Canadian Rockies from Montana. We chugged along in the rarefied air on the aptly named Going-to-the-Sun Road. As Michael and I climbed the mountain pass, the sky darkened, the trees thinned, then disappeared altogether, and suddenly it began to hail, pelting our bare arms and faces with chunks of ice the size of pea gravel. We reached the top, nothing but tundra, and snow began to fall, coating our helmets, boots, and blue jeans with a thick wet crust. As we descended the mountain and crossed the international border, the late afternoon sun shone between the jagged peaks of the Rockies, bright and pure. By the time we reached the valley into Canada, the snow had melted from our bodies and our bikes and it was summer again.

But those days are long gone. That face-to-the-wind vitality seems to have run out. My beard turns gray, the flesh on my face begins to sag, my grip slackens, and midlife doubt knocks at my door, delivering questions about career and fortune and . . . *destiny*. Is this what a midlife crisis is supposed to feel like? I don't want a red sports car, don't want a younger wife. Just some meaning, a few answers. A little wisdom would be nice.

I pick the Magic 8 Ball from my desk and give it a shake. "What's next?" I ask.

"Reply hazy, try again," it reads.

The day unwinds. School's out and Cathy files through the back door, followed by Emma, the happy kindergartner.

"I made some new friends but I can't remember all their names," Emma says, out of breath, dropping her backpack on the floor. "One girl has blonde hair and one has black hair and one has hair sorta like me. And we played kick ball in the gym and we colored. And I colored *this* for you and Mommy." She holds out a drawing, a self-portrait, Emma with rainbow hair and a half-moon smile. She dances a victory dance in the middle of the dining room, kicking up her Mary Janes and swinging her French braid against her shoulders.

"I can't wait till tomorrow," she says.

"Well, I can't either," I say, and I take her hands and join the dance, spinning her in circles.

An hour later, Ben clumps through the front door. His backpack is bulging with textbooks, his stomach is empty.

"What's to eat?" he asks as he heads for the pantry.

There's a jaunty bounce in his step. Though he doesn't dance around the dining room, he apparently has put his high school walk to rest for the time being. The makeup that hid the zit on his nose has long been wiped away, but he doesn't seem to care. His high school premiere was successful, hassle free, we're glad to hear.

"So how'd it go, how were your classes?" asks Cathy.

"Great, really great," he says, sitting at the kitchen table with a glass of milk and a slice of carrot cake.

I lean against the counter, up from my basement office, thankful to take a break from my work. "How do you like your teachers?" I ask, cutting myself a piece of cake.

"My math teacher is really cool," Ben says. "He had the Grateful Dead playing as we came into the room."

"Oh, terrific," I say. "But did you learn any math?"

"It's gonna be hard. I found out that I'm, like, the only ninth grader taking precalculus. The teacher took attendance and looked at me and said, 'Uh oh, we've got a *freshman* in here.' Pretty embarrassing."

Cathy smiles proudly. "And how about your other classes?" she asks.

"My Spanish teacher is just okay. And my physics teacher is kind of weird, typical science teacher. Sort of a nerd, and he scratches himself in front of the whole class."

I shake my head but hold my tongue, not wanting to interrupt.

"Mr. Santiago is my English teacher, he's the only minority teacher I've got. He's twenty-four and just got out of college, really psyched about teaching. We're going to start reading *Call of the Wild* by Jack London. Then we'll read *Romeo and Juliet*, *A Christmas Carol*, and a book about Vietnam. And art class is going to be pretty cool, too. We're going to be doing pottery."

Ben finishes his glass of milk and unzips his backpack.

"A lot of my teachers are, like, old hippies," he says, stacking his textbooks on the table. "My history teacher says he had hair halfway down his back when he first started teaching twenty years ago."

"It's amazing, isn't it, that these geezers can actually still hold jobs," I say, but he won't be baited by my sarcasm. He unfolds his class schedule and begins to page through his books. And as he talks, I become confident that his passage into high school will be a smooth one, certainly much smoother than mine.

I think back to my first year of high school. New Berlin High was a suburban school, bordered by shrinking farms and new home developments sprouting from cornfields. The school grounds were expansive, football field and grandstand, cinder running track, three baseball diamonds, tennis courts, acres of open fields beyond, and a wide-open sky all around. A flagpole rose in front of the school, above a broad front lawn, where students sat and ate lunch or tossed Frisbees on warm spring days. Except for a handful of foreign exchange students, the student population was entirely white—middle-class kids from the surrounding farms and developments who were bused to school from as far as fifteen miles away. The teaching staff was mostly young, just a few years out of college, the women in miniskirts and wire-rimmed glasses, the men with beards and mustaches. They talked about the current events, topical events that could not be ignored.

In the year I was a freshman, 1967, America was deep in discord. Vietnam, the civil rights movement, women's rights. A growing sense of "us versus them" pervaded college campuses, high school classrooms, and family living rooms.

For a fourteen-year-old boy, it was a confusing and contradictory time. Vince Lombardi's Green Bay Packers, my boyhood heroes, won the Superbowl—and race riots erupted in Detroit and Newark. Sex symbols Sophia Loren and Brigitte Bardot were still a boy's favored fantasies—and "women's libbers" burned bras at protest demonstrations. Riding a friend's minibike along the wooded country trails was still a favorite weekend pastime—and students were teargassed fifty miles away in Madison. Gradually, as the changes reached closer to home, as the war in Vietnam became prime-time viewing and as civil rights workers marched through the streets of Milwaukee, the turbulence of the times collided with my mood-altering hormones, and I dug in my heels in a perpetual state of rebelliousness.

The moment I hit high school, my grades began to drop in algebra, science, and even English, always my best subject. Homework assignments, tests, and term papers seemed irrelevant. I began spending less time at home, more time with my friends. My parents and I disagreed about everything—the classes I took, the clothes I wore, the radio station I listened to. At school dances, the gymnasium was transformed into a psychedelic light show by rock bands. Seniors talked of enlisting on their eighteenth birthdays or moving to Canada after graduation to avoid the draft. Stories circulated about upperclassmen selling dope. There were so many distractions. There was so much going on besides school.

Ben survives his first week of high school without incident; nobody hoists him into a drinking fountain. Already he has made new friends, a second circle of friends—*unusual* kids, polite and smart, most of them older by a year or two. He tells us about Megan, a brainy girl who wants to be a doctor and work overseas with the Red Cross. Megan lives with her mother and grandmother in a big house a few blocks away. She and Ben have been walking home from school together, trading opinions about their teachers and classes, about movies they've seen and books they've read. And there's Anton, whose parents met in South America during the sixties when they were in the Peace Corps. Anton is a talented young artist in Ben's class. Some of his paintings and sculptures are displayed in the school library, moody, abstract pieces.

Ben's newfound companions have given him new things to think about, ideas that his parents are unable to furnish.

"I think I'm going to join the debate team," he says, dropping into the sofa. "The team travels around to different schools in the area and last year they went to the state competitions. Megan's on the team and said it's hard work, but you get pretty good at arguing."

"Sounds perfect for a kid with an opinion on just about everything," I say.

"I wonder where *that* comes from," he answers, not missing a beat. Rays of afternoon light catch him in the eye. He leans sideways to dodge the brightness, and I detect a trace of a whisker above his lip.

Ben is enlivened by high school and he likes talking about it. "Then next semester I'm going to join forensics. And Pete and I might try out for the golf team in the spring. Oh yeah, and my application was accepted by the school newspaper, the *Cardinal News*. We had a staff meeting after school today."

"Hey, congratulations, that's great," I say.

"And I already have an assignment," he goes on. "The editor asked me to interview the principal and write an article for the next issue." He looks at me. "Could you help me come up with some questions?"

"Sure, sure, I'd be glad to. We'll type out a list of questions on the computer. And after you do the interview, I'll show you how to put together an article. It'll be good for you, good for both of us. We'll have fun."

I'm happy he asked me to guide him, to show him the ropes, pass along skills that I've learned in my years as a reporter. Journalism is important work, honorable work. But I'm of two minds about this as a possible career for Ben. Naturally, I'm proud to see him follow in my footsteps. On the other hand, I don't know how far I want to lead him. I would hope to see him pursue a field that's both challenging *and* lucrative. Like neurosurgery. Or professional wrestling. If he *does* decide one day to become a sculptor or a performance artist—or a writer—it would help to have (and here come the words of my father to haunt me) *something to fall back on.* An MBA or stock in an Internet start-up would help.

My father passed on a different set of skills, the skills of a carpenter. He taught me how to use his tools—a level, a nail punch, a claw hammer—tools that require patience and dexterity, care and precision. He taught me how to repair window screens, lay floor tile, caulk rain gutters, pour concrete—everything from basic plumbing to electrical work. When I was only six years old, I stood at his side on planks of scaffolding, helping him lay bricks into place on our new suburban home. Yet never did he ask if I wanted to go into his line of work, to join his business—and never did I volunteer. The subject simply wasn't discussed. Years later, my mother told me that he didn't want his sons to feel obligated to follow in his trade, as tough a life as it was, but he would have gladly welcomed an offer from any of us to join his business.

I benefited from my father's lessons. I even made a living for a short time as a handyman for hire, hanging storm doors, replacing kitchen countertops, installing shower stalls, building wooden decks and fences. It was good work, hard but satisfying. Yet I did everything I could to avoid following in my father's footsteps. I had my own path to take, I told myself.

* * *

The telephone rings. It's a call for Ben from his new friend Megan. He takes the cordless phone into his bedroom and sits on his bed, big sneakers on the quilt, pillow propped behind his back, phone in one hand and a chocolate chip cookie in the other. As I walk past his open door, I overhear a part of his conversation. He is telling his friend about his dreams of the future.

"See, I want to go to film school someday, some school out of state, I don't know where. And then I'll maybe work at a studio, just doing anything to get started. And someday I'll make my own movie.

"Or maybe I'll move to New York or somewhere and go to culinary school, become a gourmet chef. That'd be cool. And in the summers I'd live in the mountains, like, in Colorado. But before I'm out of high school, I want to spend a year in another country, maybe in South America, or France, just for a while, just to see what it's like . . ."

His ideas are wonderfully extravagant, pure, twitching impulses, the stuff teenage dreams are made of. Though his high school life is just days underway, Ben is filled with an unbridled eagerness as he rides the cusp between childhood and adulthood, the lure of independence pulling at him already with a promise to one day lead him away.

Wheels

The house is quiet as Ben and I step through the back door and into the kitchen. A grocery list scrawled in Cathy's hand sits on the dining room table, left behind in the flurry of Saturday morning errands. On a corner desk, a red light blinks eagerly on the answering machine.

"It's probably for you," I say, and I leaf through a stack of mail lying on the table. The phone never stops ringing now that Ben is in high school. It's hard for me to keep up with all of the names: Pete, Dan, Chris . . . I've known most of his buddies since they all were in middle school. They'll often crowd into our living room to watch rented videos together. But now there are the girls, Eliza, Megan, Julia—still names without faces, high, nervous voices on the telephone.

The rubber soles of Ben's oversize sneakers slap on the wooden floor as he walks through the room. He punches the play button on the phone machine, looking for something to do on a sunny Saturday. But the message is from an old friend of mine.

"Bob here," says a familiar voice. "Tim and I are heading up to the cabin for the weekend and we think you and Ben ought to come along. We can do some hiking, swimming. Hang out for a couple of days, just you, me, and the boys."

I like the sound of it: *you, me, and the boys*. Bob's fourteen-year-old son, my fourteen-year-old son, and two dads who have known each other since John Glenn circled the planet the first time.

"What do you think, Ben? Think you can tear yourself away from your friends for a weekend?"

"You ever been up to their cabin?" he asks.

"No, never have. It's on a lake, I know that much. Somewhere on the Wisconsin–Michigan state line, way up there in the north woods."

He twists his mouth, considers the prospect. "Sure. I haven't seen Timmy for a while."

I'm already sold on the idea. I could use a diversion. I call Bob's number to make plans.

"I've got to check with Cathy, but I think you can count us in," I tell him. Guys need to be with guys sometimes, and Bob's invitation is just the excuse Ben and I need to hit the road.

The plans are loose: We'll swim in Anderson Lake, canoe the Ontonagon River, take our meals when we're hungry, build an open campfire, and search the night sky for satellites and flying saucers.

"Hey, and one more thing," Bob says, "Tim says to tell Ben there's a couple of dirt bikes up there that they can ride."

I pause. "All right, I'll let him know. We'll see you soon."

I hang up the phone. Ben reaches for a shiny green apple in a bowl on the dining room table, inspects it for a second, gives it a cursory swipe across the front of his shirt, and takes a big, juicy bite.

"Bob's got some great ideas for the trip," I tell Ben. "And Tim said something about motorcycles at the cabin."

"Oh yeah? Cool," he says, his eyes as big as headlights. Motorcycles are loud and fast and dangerous, the mother of all nightmares to mothers of all ages—which makes them all the more tempting to a fourteen-year-old boy.

Late at night on the following Friday, Bob turns off a county highway just outside of Land O' Lakes, Wisconsin. The lights of his station wagon dance wildly on the trees as the four of us bump along a washboard dirt road leading into the black forest. At the very end of the road stands a white clapboard house. The cabin has been in Bob's family for decades, built by his uncle. It sits on the quiet shores of Anderson Lake. The key to the padlocked front door hangs on a nail in a toolshed, and we let ourselves in.

"Welcome to our humble little house in the woods," says Bob. He swings open the door and switches on a light. A huge stone fireplace dominates the living room, and I half expect to see the head of a buck or moose mounted above the mantel. But as I look around the cabin, I see that it's more of a country inn than a hunting lodge. The kitchen is framed by knotty-pine cabinets, stocked with a full complement of pots and pans, a microwave, even a popcorn popper. Three bedrooms are furnished with bunk beds.

"This place is great," says Ben, inspecting the rooms. "Running water, bunk beds, TV, a VCR, and everything. I thought we'd be, like, sleeping on the floor and using an outhouse or something."

We unpack the car, piling our duffel bags and hiking boots in the center of the kitchen. Outside, the cry of a loon from the lake interrupts the midnight stillness, and the four of us walk down to a wooden pier to listen. Stars pierce the inky blue sky. Moonlight and bug lights from a distant cabin reflect off the water, and the low warble of a second loon echoes the first: *oooo-WHOOOO*. The first loon answers, the second replies, and a third joins in, then a fourth, and suddenly we are serenaded in full stereo by the sound of dozens of loons composing their mating calls in the thick summer air. Then, abruptly, as if on cue, the symphony comes to a crescendo and stops. It's dead quiet.

"Loony tunes," says Bob, breaking the holy silence. Ben and Tim groan, and we tramp back to the cabin to sleep.

We rise early the next morning. I open a door off the kitchen and step onto a wide screened porch. Coffee cup in hand, I sit in a lumpy overstuffed armchair and listen. Someone cuts firewood with a chainsaw far away. A fish breaks the surface of the lake. A hummingbird hovers at a feeder just beyond the screen, drawing sweet water into its needle-thin beak, the flutter of its blurred wings not making a sound.

Bob and I fix a quick breakfast of cold cereal, toast, and orange juice for the four of us, and as we eat, the boys swap stories about the new school year and the teachers they already hate.

"My history teacher is a real dork," says Tim as he sips the milk from the bottom of his cereal bowl. "He's got this little sign on his desk that says something like 'The only thing new in the world is the history that *you don't know*.'"

Ben and Tim have known each other most of their lives. But as with Bob and me, their friendship flourishes only when their paths cross, which isn't very often. While Tim is just five months younger than Ben, he started school a year later. Yet in appearance, the two are replicas. Both wear baseball caps, floppy khaki shorts that hang past their knees, and untucked T-shirts. They also have the same hairstyle—buzzed in the back like an aborted Marine Corps cut, parted in the middle and falling to both sides of their foreheads. Ben's hair is darker and his limbs are shorter and thicker than Tim's, each boy a reflection of his father's genes.

I lean back in my chair at the wooden kitchen table, considering the sun as it glances off the lake.

"It's gonna be a golden day," Bob declares as he empties the coffeepot.

Right now, I'm happy to let the day begin without me. I would be perfectly content to waste away a couple of hours on the screened porch with a book, then take a swim before lunch. But the boys have other ideas. Like pups sniffing at the front door, they're ready for action, movement, adventure, *fun*.

"C'mon, let's go," Tim says. "I want to show Ben how to ride the dirt bike."

Ben has never operated a motorcycle before. A city boy, his sets of wheels have been bicycles, scooters, in-line skates—nothing motorized, toys compared to a motorcycle.

I've ridden a number of motorcycles; I've owned three. For a year or so, before I was married, a motorcycle was my sole source of transportation. I lived in Colorado at the time and rode year-round, rain or shine, stubbornly refusing to buy a car, playing up the image of the "Iron Ass," as Cathy called me, sliding recklessly over ice-glazed highways or splashing along streets flooded by early summer thunderstorms. Today I limp around in an old four-wheel-drive Subaru station wagon, a leftover from our Colorado days, while Cathy drives a Volvo (Grateful Dead sticker in the back window), bought as a family car because of its reputation for being safe.

Ben pulls open the front door and marches outside with Tim.

"I guess we don't have a choice," says Bob, and he grabs a flannel shirt from the back of a chair. We follow the boys out. The sky is clear, the air is dry. The sun burns through the trees and lights patches of green and brown all around us. The boys roll two cycles out of the shed and onto the dirt driveway. They're both small bikes, low to the ground, four-speed Yamaha 80s, silver and black with a red slash across the gas tank. Tim hands Ben a silver helmet. A few nicks mark the gleaming sparkle finish. Ben pulls it over his head and pushes his brown bangs under the shell. He fumbles with the chin strap.

"Here, let me show you," I say. I step up and thread the black strap through the metal ring under his chin, then thump him on his head with the flat of my hand.

Tim pushes up the kickstand on his bike and throws a leg confidently over the seat. He digs his toes into the dirt and pushes his bike ahead of Ben's a few feet, facing the road. He balances with no hands, completely at ease. Taking Tim's cue, Ben steadies his own bike, one hand on the handlebar, one on the leather seat, and pushes up the kickstand with the toe of his sneaker. The bike begins to fall away from him, but he grabs on. Placing both hands on the grips, he swings a leg over the seat and plants himself squarely in the saddle, rocking the bike left and right between his legs, feeling its heaviness.

39

"So far, so good," I say. It's just a small bike, with a small engine, I tell myself. But I'm not convinced. Motorcycles, large or small, can be as hazardous as they are exciting. I'm not sure I want Ben to discover either effect.

I huddle next to him and begin spitting out instructions.

"Okay. Turn the key to the right." A green light shines on the instrument panel beneath the speedometer. "Good. Now, left foot, rear brake. Right hand, front brake," I say, sounding like a Dr. Seuss book. "The left hand is the clutch. You shift gears with your right foot. It's in neutral. So pull in the clutch and give it a try."

"This one?" he asks, confused.

"Yep, left is the clutch."

Ben tugs at the clutch lever with his fingers and pushes down on the shifter, clicking through the gears. He studies the controls, concentrating hard, as if he's working out a math problem.

"The kick-start is on the left side," Tim says, pointing with his toe. He kicks it once, twice, twists the accelerator, kicks once again, and the engine fires up. The cracking sound disturbs the morning quiet. Blue smoke belches from the single exhaust pipe behind the rear tire.

"Go ahead, Ben, start it up."

Ben looks at his feet, steals a glance at me, then looks down at the bike again. He grits his teeth and places his foot on the kick-start. Compared to Tim, Ben looks rather uncertain.

"Think you can do it?" I ask him, and suddenly the father in me, the guardian, sees Ben spread-eagled under a tree, blood on his forehead, limbs bent at unnatural angles. I imagine his mother's voice over the telephone, breaking into tiny sobs as I deliver the grim news: "The doctors are confident he'll be out of the cast by Thanksgiving . . ."

I shake away the image and stand back, crossing my arms against my chest and rocking on the heels of my hiking boots. With "Born to Be Wild" playing in the back of my mind and the conscience of Ben's more sensible parent perched on my shoulder like some Saturday morning cartoon character, I watch him kick the mechanical beast to life.

The bike starts on the second kick. Ben keeps a serious face, winding the engine with the accelerator. And with the first pop of the engine, like a gunshot, the father figure in me disappears, the guardian is gone, and I stare at Ben as if it were *me* on the seat, tightening my hands around the spongy rubber handle grips, testing the bounce of the shock absorbers with my weight. I can smell the fumes of gasoline rising from the guts of the bike, taste the invincibility on Ben's breath, and see freedom dancing in his eyes—an open road, a burst of speed, a fist raised to the sky . . .

I first learned to ride a motorcycle with Bob. We were each about the age of Ben and Tim, maybe a year younger, when our friend Danny bought a Honda 90 with money he'd earned from his paper route. It was a used bike, the paint on the black-and-silver gas tank pitted and chipped, the chrome exhaust pipe scorched metallic blue by the heat of the engine. But what a thrill it was climbing on top of that machine for the first time! Squeezing the cushioned seat with my legs, I looked at myself in the round mirror, no helmet, thick dark hair hanging over my glasses, a careless grin stretched across my face.

We took turns speeding around Danny's half-acre yard with hardly a hint of how to stop the thing. Right palm on the throttle, pop the clutch—it was all we needed to know. A dizzying rush of speed and power, the neck-snapping torque was a perfect supplement to the testosterone coursing through our teenage veins. Though we probably never topped thirty miles per hour, I felt as if I had absolute control of my life for the first time.

More than once, though, it was all too much to handle, even at thirty miles per hour. I would miss a gear or mistake the brake for the clutch and go sailing over the handlebars, head over heels, tumbling onto the hard lawn as the machine sputtered and died.

But each time I fell, I got up, shook the ringing from my ears, and tried again, more worried about harming the bike than my body.

Like a fool, I mentioned the bike to my parents. They immediately forbade me from ever riding it again.

"You don't have a license for that thing," my father said.

"Do you wear a helmet? What if you get hurt?" my mother lamented, concerned about both my well-being and the possibility of a large hospital bill. I rode anyway, giddy with defiance, speeding along the trails in the woods near Danny's house and down the gravel roads of his subdivision, a white cloud of dust in my wake. My parents didn't understand motorcycles, I told myself. No one was going to get hurt. It was all for the thrill, the release. My father never rode a motorcycle. What did he know?

Years later, a motorcycle was my instrument of escape when I left my parents' home once and for all. I was twenty-one when I strapped a tattered knapsack to the back of my Honda 550, tucked my ponytail into my leather bomber jacket, and pointed the front tire west. Like so many other young men and women at the time, my exodus was urgent. I yearned for a drink of the world, and my hometown could no longer quench my thirst. On my departure day, my father held out his right hand, wishing me farewell in that manful but mournful way that says "I hope you know what you're doing." Away I rode, across the Midwestern plains to the Rocky Mountains, in search of something more.

Motorcycles were independence, flight, rebellion, a disregard for convention. A sneering Dennis Hopper in *Easy Rider*, giving the finger to the rednecks in the pickup. I've been reckless on a motorcycle, and I've been just plain stupid. I remember driving at night, drunk on bourbon and beer, on a narrow highway through Oregon logging country (or maybe it was northern California). I switched off my headlight and rode in pitch blackness so I could follow the stars of the Milky Way overhead.

Ben sits on top of the Yamaha, eager to get going. The engine snaps like firecrackers. I'm tempted to rip the key from the ignition and toss it into the lake, forbidding him forever from riding one of these risky machines. I might as well be placing a cigarette to his lips and lighting the match, inviting him to gamble with his life. But I have little justification for denying him the thrill, and he has figured this out. He's listened to my travel stories, and as with most of the life experiences he's heard me talk about, he believes he has a license, a *right*, to experience at least what I have, and maybe more. If I protest, he can fairly label me a hypocrite. He has me, he *knows* he has me, and I *know* he knows.

"Okay," I say, tugging nervously at my beard. "Watch out for the exhaust pipe next to your leg. It gets hot. Pull out slow. Don't give it too much gas."

Ben starts down the road, rolling, jerking, nearly stalling the engine. He gives it more gas and the wheels spin in the dirt. He creeps along for twenty or thirty yards, just fast enough to balance on two wheels, then stops, pulls in the clutch, turns around, and stops again. He returns to where Bob and I are standing and repeats the pattern, Tim leading him along, twisting around on his seat to watch.

"Keep your foot on the brake," I yell to Ben. "Easy, easy."

I run alongside Ben's bike for a couple of passes, guiding him toward the center of the road, telling him when to shift, cautioning him on his speed. Diligently and excitedly, he begins to master the rhythm—foot on the brake, out with the clutch, gas to the engine. Brake, clutch, gas. Brake, clutch, gas, a smooth synchronization. And slowly, under the yellow-green canopy of elm and oak and birch, with flecks of sunlight dappled on his young face, he takes control.

I think back a few years to a shady lane in front of our home in Minneapolis. I'm holding onto the handlebar of a black-and-silver bicycle, guiding Ben down the street, my feet hitting the pavement in cadence with the revolving rubber wheels, running, spinning, running, until Ben is pedaling frantically on his own. On this dusty backwoods road in Wisconsin, a different force is

43

driving him, a force both combustible and chemical. Try as I might as I run to keep up, I am no match. All I can do is watch as he lurches ahead of me. Brake, clutch, gas.

"They're off and running," Bob says, and the two boys ride out of our sight.

"Jesus, I don't know," I shake my head. "Maybe I should ride along on the back or something. He looked pretty shaky to me."

"You'd make him so nervous he'd crash into a tree," Bob says. "He's doing okay. Sometimes you just have to let 'em go."

We sit down on the grass at the side of the road and wait.

Bob and I grew up in the community of New Berlin, a rural suburb west of Milwaukee, in a development of streets named after explorers: Magellan Drive, DeSoto Lane, Balboa Drive. We met in the third grade at Elmwood Elementary. Bob was a runty kid with a cowlick that shot up above his forehead; the girls at school called him cute. I wasn't so lucky. I wore brown-rimmed glasses that, with my dark hair, made me look slightly Asian. Boys in my class would pull at the corners of their eyes, thrust out their top teeth, and make bogus Chinese sounds: "Ah *so*, ah *so!*" Bob would try not to laugh, try to be my ally, but peer pressure got the better of him and he joined in the teasing.

I had lived in Milwaukee proper until I was five, when my parents fled the city, seeking a vegetable garden and more room to breathe. I remember standing in the backyard of our new home on a February afternoon shortly after moving day, wrapped in a blue fleece snowsuit, black rubber boots, and a red wool scarf, staring at the overcast sky as it met the snow-covered pastureland-turned-subdivision. There was no horizon. There was no sound, no movement, no people. I had been dropped from the sky onto a lifeless planet.

In the city, I had been able to walk to my kindergarten class, walk to the candy story across from school for licorice sticks and candy corn. In the city, my mother could do her shopping at the local bakery and butcher shop and grocery store. But in our pastureland neighborhood, where there were no sidewalks, wheels were compulsory. Wheels of the long yellow school bus took me to school. Wheels of my mother's big cream-colored Mercury took me to Cub Scout meetings, to my grandmother's house, to St. Mary's church, to the drive-through bank.

For Bob and I, our bicycles were our tickets to new worlds. With baseball cards clamped to the spokes with clothespins and colored streamers spraying from the grips, we would ride out of our mothers' sight to Kelly's Pond a mile away, where the air smelled like snakes on humid days. There, we'd roll up our pants and wade barefoot through the cattails, catching frogs and tadpoles and salamanders with our hands and holding them captive for a day or two in mayonnaise jars so we could examine them. When we were a few years older, we would pedal to the neighboring town of Hales Corners and one of the first strip malls in the area. We would cruise through the vast parking lots, dodging cars and shopping carts on our obstacle course, and stop at the five-and-dime to buy candy cigarettes and waxed candy lips or to see if the latest Hardy Boys mystery had come in.

My first bicycle was second-hand, a twenty-inch. It was rusty and banged up when I got it, a homely brown with white trim. The left pedal clapped on the chain guard, and the tires rubbed on the bent fenders. I was embarrassed to take it out of the garage. Over winter when I was eight or nine, I disassembled the bike in the basement with my father's help. We removed the handlebars, fenders, wheels, and seat. We soaked the chain in gasoline to dissolve the gritty black grease. We sanded away the rust and spray-painted the frame with a double coat of glossy black. The wheel frames I painted silver. I added new tires, high handlebars, and a long white seat. By springtime, it was a new ride. I pedaled to the top of what was known as Hollywood Hill and sped through the subdivision for all my friends to see. Most of them, including Bob, had new store-bought bikes with high-gloss finishes and chrome wheels, but I was proud of what I had made with my father that winter in the basement.

For my tenth birthday, my parents bought me a new bike, a three-speed twenty-six-inch Schwinn, ocean blue, with chrome fenders, a generator-powered headlight, and a red taillight. The bike was a surprise. My father rolled it onto the backyard patio during my birthday party. I shined it every weekend with Turtle Wax and wiped the thing dry with a chamois every time I got caught in the rain. I was the envy of Hales Heights Estates, pedaling through the subdivision. Then one day my friend Donald's tenth birthday came around. He got a fire-engine red ten-speed with English racer handlebars that swooped down to his knees, and I was no longer King of the Road.

I took too many chances with my Schwinn, and accidents were many. Fresh tar and gravel were applied to the roads each summer, making bike travel almost impossible. One day, on my way home from Bob's house, I sped down Hollywood Hill late for dinner and missed the turn onto my street. I slid sideways at the bottom of the hill, both tires scattering sheets of gravel as I fought to make the turn, my bike going one way and me going another. I ended up sprawled on the neighbor's lawn, my bike in the drainage ditch. With my knees and elbows bloodied and wet, I hobbled home, pushing my bike at my side.

My mother washed away the blood and dabbed orange Mercurochrome onto my cuts and scrapes. Then I went outside to inspect my bike.

"You've got to be more careful," my father said to me in the garage. He took his toolbox from his truck and helped me straighten the handlebars and fenders. Some of the damage could not be fixed. Looking back, I'm sure he was as disappointed as I was to see that the new bike had been marred. But as he ran his hand over the scratched chain guard and dented headlamp, he hid his feelings behind a stern face, not saying anything more.

* * *

The dirt bikes buzz like insects in the distance, louder and louder until Ben and Tim emerge from around a bend. Ben gently squeezes the hand brake and rolls to a stop five feet from me. His hands rest comfortably on the grips. He smiles a Cheshire cat smile.

Bob and I are on our feet. "Well, how'd it go?" I ask. I take hold of Ben's handlebar to steady him as he shifts the bike into neutral.

"Pretty good," he says, his bike still running, ready for more. "I never got out of second gear. I still can't shift very well. But it feels good." His helmet is pushed back on his forehead and the strap has loosened. He's intact.

"He did great," Tim agrees. "We weren't really going very fast."

"These bikes are good for learning," adds Bob. "It's hard to mess up."

Ben looks down at the bike, admiring the sleek shape of the gas tank, the shiny chrome exhaust pipe. He revs the engine just to make noise. He's pleased with his first ride.

Tim kills the power to his bike and dismounts, leaping off the seat. But instead of dropping the kickstand, he offers the bike to me.

"You want to take it for a ride?"

I take the handlebar. The last motorcycle I owned was a 750cc BMW, silver and blue, a beautifully crafted machine made for the open road. I put more than twenty-five thousand miles on the bike, then sold it just before Cathy and I married, a heartbreaking but unavoidable decision. We needed a car, and a BMW touring bike was not the most practical way to haul groceries. With the money, we bought an old Mercedes Benz that we nicknamed Puff because it burned oil so badly. I promised myself I'd get another bike someday, but Cathy and I began raising children, and fatherhood and motorcycles never seemed to be a responsible combination.

I climb onto Tim's bike and start the engine with a single kick. The vibration beneath me is familiar, exhilarating, sensual, but the bike is miniature, boyish, a plaything, even smaller than

Danny's old Honda 90. I pull a pair of aviator sunglasses from my pocket and wipe them across my pants leg. Tim tosses his helmet at me. On these back roads, a helmet seems unnecessary, but I squeeze it over my head. Don't want to be a bad role model. When I glance into the side mirror, I see not the young upstart that I once was, not the rugged Iron Ass in a leather jacket who rode the highways coast to coast. I see some old guy in a polo shirt with specks of white in his beard—Ben's dad with a helmet on.

"Okay, Captain America," says Bob. "We'll call the state patrol if you're not back by dark." And he gives us a thumbs up.

"Which way?" Ben asks. I motion in the direction of the county highway. "Straight ahead, out to the highway and back."

I test the brakes, pull in the clutch, and check all four gears as the bike idles. Then I give Ben a nod and pull away. The engine whines as I let out the clutch too slow, but by the time I'm in third gear, my reflexes are revived and the bike is mine.

The curves tighten as we weave through the forest. The waters of Anderson Lake glisten to our right. I catch glimpses of Ben in my mirror, leaning tentatively into the narrow turns, his eyes panning the dirt road. He looks tiny in my mirror, bumping behind me as if I'm towing him with an invisible rope. Dirt turns to asphalt and a long paved straightaway. My speedometer reads thirty-five miles per hour. A car passes us and Ben hugs the shoulder. Good. Good to be cautious, I tell him silently.

We whirl along the pavement, the engines echoing under the overhanging trees. My hands are numbed by the vibration. My shirttail whips behind me in the breeze. The little Yamaha bucks as I shift, rocking me on the seat as we move through shafts of sunlight. When we reach the highway, I'm tempted for a second to keep on going, to run it through the gears on the open road. But I brake at the stop sign, make a slow U-turn, and park along the shoulder. Ben follows in my track, leaning into the half-circle as he makes his turn. He rolls up to my side and stops. The Cheshire cat smile reappears.

"So how does it feel?" I say.

Ben shifts his bike into neutral before he answers. "It's great, it's fun, really fun. It was kind of bumpy and I almost lost my grip back on the dirt, but I think I'm getting the hang of it. I got it into third gear." He caresses the shiny gas tank. "I can see where I might want to get one of these things someday."

The bug. Already he's bitten.

"Not while your mother's still breathing," I joke. But I drift away for a minute on a daydream: Ben and me riding down a highway together, trees rushing by, white billowing clouds in the distance, blue sky above.

I kick the dirt bike into gear and give the accelerator a quick twist. It replies with a pop, ready to go. I wish the bike were larger, I tell myself, more of a motorcycle. But the sensation is irresistible.

"All *right*," I smile, and I start back down the road toward the cabin, making room to my right for Ben to ride alongside. My feet rest solidly on the foot pegs; my hands palm the handle grips. As I accelerate, the engine grabs from below, tugging at my body; my arms are fully extended, my back straight. This is the best way to travel, the purest form of freedom I know. Complete mechanical might, all senses bare to the elements.

As we glide along the straightaway, I decide that I'm moving too slowly. I want more speed. No one's around. The road is dry. This bike is a miniature, but I want to know how fast it will go. Rock 'n' roll starts playing in my head, electric, a swelling, rumbling beat . . . and I break away from Ben, shifting quickly through all the gears—one, two, three, four—pushing the speedometer up to forty, fifty, sixty miles per hour. The speed snaps my head, caves in my chest. I dip a shoulder to the right, bank into a wide curve, and I lose Ben. I forget about my fatherly role, my responsibility. My eyes glisten as the wind whips my face, and I'm carried away.

I reach the end of the asphalt sooner than I expect and bounce onto the washboard, thumping on the deep grooves in the dirt. I'm taken off guard, and my feet are jarred loose from the pegs. They dangle in the air, and I feel like an amateur, out of control. The road bends sharply to the left, and I realize I'm going much too fast. I check my mirror, hoping Ben isn't on my tail. I don't see him. But when I look up, I'm heading into the path of a blazing, moving mass of red. I find the back brake lever with my toe and push down hard, then yank back on the front brake, swinging all of my weight to the right, trying to pitch the bike back into the right lane. Right shoulder down, knee flared wide. But it's too much, too much weight shifting at one time. I overcorrect, and my rear tire starts to break loose in the dirt.

The red mass veers to its right, honks, and blurs by, missing me by just three or four feet. With knees locked and both legs extended to the ground, I catch my balance for an instant and try to pivot on a heel. But I'm still moving too fast and, with my foot again off the rear brake, I fly into the woods, crashing over ferns and dogwood and deadfall. My right hand grabs the brake lever, but the front tire rams into the bare trunk of an elm tree. I'm launched into the air, my legs spread-eagled, my equilibrium lost. In slow motion, I lose my grasp on the handle grips and jam my right foot into the dirt, hunched and off kilter, my left leg swinging, spinning, dancing in a half circle.

The engine sputters and the bike falls away to my left. I hit the ground with a hard jolt, sitting straight up in the weeds. The Iron Ass is flat on his ass.

Silence except for the uneven jangle of the bike's hot engine as it cools.

Seconds or hours later, I hear the sound of Ben's bike grinding through the forest. It speeds up, slows down, shuts off. I want to hide, bury myself in leaves, or run into the bog and away from this *trouble*. But instead, I lay on my back and stare at the clouds, trapped in my folly. My helmet is pushed over my eyes. My sunglasses hang at my chin from one ear.

Ben tromps through the underbrush and stands over me, dumbfounded. "What happened to *you*? What are you doing *here*?"

"Nothing, nothing," I say, content to remain motionless for a while, afraid that I've blown out a knee or thrown out my back. "Thought I'd just lie here and die, that's all."

Ben can see that I'm not injured. No blood spilled, no metal twisted, no flames shooting from the bike.

"Dad, Dad, Dad," he shakes his head. "Looks like Captain America wiped out, huh."

"It looks that way, huh." And suddenly I'm back at Danny's house, explaining to my jeering buddies how I ended up once again flat on the ground with mud on my face.

Ben sits in the grass without saying a word and loosens the strap on his helmet. He balls up a green leaf in the palm of his hand and tosses it at me, hitting me in the face. He laughs. I try to sit up. I shoot him a scowl.

"Well, give me hand. Help your old man up." He stands, reaches out, grabs my left hand, and slowly pulls me to my feet. I dust myself off and inspect the Yamaha. The mirrors need adjusting, and weeds are protruding from the headlight and fender, but there's no damage to the bike, and no damage to me. Except for the gaping dent in my pride.

I pull my helmet off and scratch the back of my head. Sunlight catches me full in the face, but I feel weak, woozy. The youthful invincibility that I had felt as I climbed into the saddle of this bike is gone. I'm supposed to be the guide here, the teacher. But it's Ben looking out for me, an odd reversal.

Ben lifts my bike from the weeds and waits.

"I think I'm done with this thing for the day," I confess, taking the handlebar. I straighten the mirrors and twist my sunglasses back into shape. "Let's head back."

Ben helps me wheel the bike back to the road. I climb on and give the starter a firm kick. The bike coughs once, whines, but

51

doesn't turn over. I try again; still no fire. A third try, and finally it comes alive with a complaining grunt. Ben hops on his bike. He draws in the clutch and starts the engine with one kick. He shifts into first, but as he begins to pull away he lets go of the clutch too quickly and the engine stalls.

"Slowly, let it out slowly," I remind him. "And give it a little more gas."

He looks at me for a long moment, doubtful, but follows my instructions. He starts the engine again, then slowly, evenly, releases the clutch lever and starts to roll down the road.

Sunlight sparkles on the chrome exhaust pipe of his bike as he pulls away. I follow behind, watching over his shoulder as he navigates the bumpy, curvy road. I fix my eyes on his round mirror, the small reflection of his face. He shifts into second, then third, and abruptly he speeds up. In his mirror, I see a half-smirk crack his face. He looks back at me through the smirk and slows for a second. But I wave him on.

"Go ahead, I'll catch up with you," I yell, knowing he can't hear. He guns the engine and disappears around a bend.

Shaving Lessons

Ben has a confession to make. Though he won't say the word *girlfriend*, there apparently is a certain young female at his school who has caught his attention. Or it may have been the other way around.

Ben sits on a stool at the kitchen table leaning over a bowl of day-old popcorn, picking out the old maids and lining them up in a row beside a glass of juice. He's just gotten off the telephone with his friend Pete, and he's talkative, feeling good about himself.

"See, there's this girl in one of my classes," he explains to his mother and me. "And I guess she asked one of Pete's friends whether I would ever, like, want to go out with her or something. So I don't know, we might do something sometime."

In one liquid movement, Cathy turns from the china cabinet where she's stacking dinner plates to the table and faces Ben.

"What do you mean?" she says, smiling as she speaks the words. "When did you hear this? When did all this come about?"

"Well . . .," he hesitates. "I don't know *exactly*. It's kind of a long story." As Cathy begins to press him for details, he now seems to have second thoughts about confessing anything more.

But it's too late. Cathy is on full alert. She slings a dish towel over her shoulder and places a hand on her hip.

"So what's her name?" I ask, trying to take a neutral side. I've just come inside from an afternoon run. My left knee has tightened up and I'm walking in circles, hobbling, trying to work it out.

"Sarah," Ben says.

Cathy twirls a curl of her brown hair between her fingers. She's nervous, as if she's just learned for the first time that Ben in fact will *not* be living at home for the rest his life. So long Oedipus, hello Venus.

Ben looks longingly from the kitchen to his open bedroom door.

"And how long have you known her, this . . . Sarah?" Cathy persists, peering into his face. "Do you like her?"

"Do I like her?" Ben repeats. "I *guess*." He gulps down the last of his drink and begins to stand.

"What's she like, Ben?" Cathy asks, and she sits on a stool next to him. He drops back down on the vinyl seat, letting out a sigh.

"Where does she live?" she continues, more casually now. "What does she look like? Tell me."

"*Mommm* . . .," and finally Ben makes his break. He stuffs a handful of popcorn into his mouth and stamps out of the kitchen.

"I was just asking," she says, looking at me innocently.

This is a marker event for her, another step in her baby boy's passage into another domain, away from hers, away from ours. I understand. I can already count the years before he leaves for college, the number of birthdays left to celebrate together, the number of baseball seasons left to enjoy together. I can't imagine the hole he'll leave when he's gone. Meanwhile, though, he should be allowed some secrecy, some room to breathe.

Cathy wonders aloud if Ben's been coming home late after school not because of meetings with the student newspaper staff, but because he's been rendezvousing with this Sarah.

Ben overhears this and shuffles back into the room, ready to explain himself.

"I have her in my English class," he says, gesturing with his hands, palms up. Though he seems a bit embarrassed, I sense that in a way he's flattered to be chosen. By a girl. And, though I don't say it, I think he's happy to have unleashed a little maternal jealousy.

We drift into the living room, where I ease myself into the rocking chair, as Cathy paces back and forth across the carpet. I feel as if I'm watching a performance, a play, with Cathy taking one of the oldest roles there is, the overprotective, solicitous mother.

Ben keeps his distance, leaning in the doorway.

"You've been getting an awful lot of phone calls lately from other girls, too, Ben," says Cathy. "Some are older than you, aren't they? Sophomores? Juniors? Why haven't we met any of them? What's going on?"

Ben closes his eyes and stalks off. "Just never mind." He withdraws to his room.

"You better talk to him," Cathy says to me, still pacing.

"About what?"

"What do you think? About girls. About sex."

"We had that talk. Years ago. You were there."

"Maybe he needs to hear it again. He's still so young. His voice hasn't changed. *Talk* to him." She walks into the kitchen.

Maybe she's right. Maybe I have my head in the sand. Because Ben is so levelheaded, I've always assumed that he'd be a reasonable teenager when it came to sex. But who am I kidding? Adolescence has nothing to do with reason.

I sit in the living room the following morning, reading the newspaper, cup of coffee on the table at my side. I turn from the front page to the opinion page, and out of the corner of my eye, across the length of the house, I see movement. I see Ben in the bathroom. The door is open and he's standing in front of the mirror. He rubs the end of his chin between his index finger and thumb, turns his head to the left to examine his profile, turns to the right, rubs again, adding more histrionics with every rub, then pats his top lip gingerly with a finger.

"Dad?" he says, without looking away from the mirror. "Do you have a razor I could borrow?"

I put down my newspaper. A razor. It has not been a word in his vocabulary until now. "Ah, let me take a look."

Ben has been unusually modest lately, rarely allowing himself to be seen around the house without a shirt on. It's a funny contrast to the same boy who ran naked through the backyard sprinkler a dozen years ago. His humility leaves me with an odd sense of loss. But I know I can't intrude on his privacy. Occasionally I catch him in his room after a shower, shirtless, and I notice five or six spindly hairs sprouting from the center of his chest and a dark patch growing under his arms. As I brush by him in our tiny bathroom, up close I can see short strands of whiskers, fine and velvety, beneath his nose and at the very end of his chin. For a second, I'm tempted to check the whiskers with my fingertips to see if they'll rub away.

I open the door to the bathroom closet. Coincidentally, a complimentary razor had arrived in the mail a week or two earlier. I stashed it at the time, thinking it might come in handy one day. With a flourish, I present it to Ben.

"Ah ha, here it is! Your first Gillette, still in the box."

The razor is plastic, lightweight, toylike, with a narrow double-bladed cartridge that pivots as it courses the dimples and clefts of a man's face, similar to the razor I use. I've worn a full beard most of my adult life but keep it closely trimmed and shave above and below it every other day.

Ben tears into the packaging and looks the razor over, turning it curiously in his hand and softly placing a finger on the blades. I can see that he's asking for a lesson, not just a tool.

I clear away the bathroom clutter from the edge of the sink— a plastic *101 Dalmatians* cup, a bottle of red nail polish, a wayward toothbrush—and run the hot water, filling the basin. I stand behind Ben and look at our images in the mirror. He's still a head shorter than I. The brown hair on his head is thick and auburn-tinted, my hair sparse on top and dusted with gray along the sides. His eyes are noticeably two different shades, one green, his mother's color, one brown, from me. His dark eyebrows dart to his temples; his chin points when he smiles. A handsome boy, a handsome man imminent.

The experience of shaving is ceremonial for a father and son, at once a clumsy farce and a triumphant rite of passage. It's an acknowledgment both of vanity and of maturity. My first shaving lesson was a private, solemn affair. My father thought I should first watch him go through the motions. I stood next to him at the sink on that particular morning, and the sweet fragrance of shaving cream mixed with his sour breath of coffee and cigarettes.

He began to lather up, spreading menthol foam on his weathered, rugged face like he was dabbing spackle on drywall. Swiftly, mechanically, he pulled the razor over his face, clearing away the stubborn foam, two passes through the lather, one with each side of the doubled-edged razor, then pausing to tap the razor's head on the porcelain sink and rinse it under hot running water. He looked at me wordlessly in the mirror, and continued until he erased the cream from each cheek. Then he lifted his head back, frowned purposely to expose the tightened skin on his neck, and ran the razor upward from his Adam's Apple to his chin. Lastly, he attacked his mustache, scraping away the whiskers in short, chopping strokes, his upper lip curled tight.

In less than a minute, he was clean shaven, leaving just small dollops of white foam under his ear lobes, nose, and chin. He dashed a handful of water on his cheeks and jowls and wiped away the remaining lather with his hand towel. For the final touch, he took a white glass bottle of Old Spice from a wooden tray on top of the toilet tank, dribbled a puddle into his palm, ran his hands together once or twice, and slapped the aftershave onto his miraculously smooth skin.

"Lather up," he said, standing beside me like a baseball coach watching a player take batting practice.

I dabbed at my chin, at my jawbone, and at my upper lip as my father put a fresh blade in the razor. He twisted the tip of the handle until the jaws of the razor yawned wide. Then, from a flat cartridge, he slid a new blade into the razor's head with his thumb.

He closed the razor and passed it me. It was heavy in my hand, shiny steel, almost a weapon. As I raised it to my face, imitating the same grimaces that he'd made into the mirror, he put his hand over mine and guided the instrument slowly across my cheek, down to my chin and back up again, steadying my hand with each sweep.

When the lather was gone, I splashed warm water on my face and my father handed his towel to me. It was still damp with shaving cream from his face. My reflection shined in the mirror, fresh, neat, but still a few years short of manful. When finally I was required to shave daily, I grew my sideburns long and cultivated a thin mustache. By the time I was twenty, I had relinquished my razor altogether.

A few weeks after my first shaving lesson, my father and I attended a school-sponsored sex education program. I knew what to expect. My friend Bob had already clued me in on the facts of life. Dutifully and boastfully, Bob reported what his two older sisters had told him about the ins and outs of sex, using as visual aids a stash of *Playboy* magazines taken from the top drawer of his father's highboy. So when my father somberly accompanied me to the sex ed program, I learned very few new details, aside from the anatomical workings of a woman's body, which at the time were immaterial to me.

"So, got any questions?" my father asked as he drove us home, glancing my way.

"Not really. Nope. Guess not," I said.

And with that briefest of discussions and my first shaving lesson, I officially graduated into puberty.

Ben opens the medicine cabinet and from behind the mirror takes out a green-and-white can of Barbasol shaving cream—"Made with Aloe," the can declares—the cream I use on my face. He removes the cap. He pushes down hard on the button, too hard, and a small blizzard of foam fills his hand and plops into the sink.

"It's just soap, don't worry about it," I say.

He begins painting his face with the cream. He has no whiskers yet on his cheeks or jaw, so he dabs only at his upper lip and chin, earnestly but carefully. He spreads too much, and most of his mouth gets covered behind a white mask.

"Yuck," he says. He smacks his lips and spits, wiping the Barbasol from the corners of his mouth.

"Doesn't taste at all like whipping cream, does it," I say. I take the razor from the edge of the sink, dip it into the filled basin, and hand it to Ben. "Careful now. You'll nick yourself if you press too hard, especially there below your nose."

He presses his top lip against his teeth, stretching taut the skin between his lip and nose, and slowly takes a single swipe at the latent mustache. It's so quiet I can almost hear the razor squeak on his young skin, and I think of a Cub Scout carnival game that Ben once played. The object was to shave the lather from an inflated red balloon. Ben played the game three or four times, carefully gliding a razor over the smooth balloon, not popping it once.

Ben stops and stares at the glass. Nothing has been removed but cream.

"You've got to angle the blade just a bit more," I say. "Let me show you."

I curl my arm over his shoulder from behind, place my hand over his hand, and position the razor on his skin. Together, we angle the plastic handle of the razor and pull down toward his lip.

We repeat the movement and look into the mirror, trying to will the mustache away. But the wispy hair remains.

Ben rinses the razor and glares at himself, unsure what's wrong with his technique. Emma appears in the doorway.

"I have to go to the bathroom," she says.

"Not now, Emma. You have to wait," Ben cuts her off, annoyed at the interruption.

She crosses her ankles and stretches her arms across the doorway, eyeing her brother suspiciously. "What's Ben doing?"

"Never *mind*, Emma," he says.

"Is Ben shaving? Does it hurt?"

I gently shoo her away. "Come back in a couple of minutes, sweetheart," I say, and I swing the bathroom door shut.

"Okay, try again, Ben, just yourself this time. You have to get the feel of the blade."

He coats his upper lip and chin with a new layer of Barbasol, playing with the suds, pulling his white foam beard to a point, and laughs once into the mirror. "I've got a goatee."

He makes another pass over his lip, and this time the blade catches, tugging gently on his skin. He taps the razor on the sink and a residue of dark, minced hair appears.

"That did it," he says happily. "It's coming off, finally." The shorn whiskers are trophies, proof of passage.

He dips the razor into the water and moves on to his chin, raising his head back, staring down his nose, running the blade over a dozen shy strands. He moves the razor with newfound faith.

The cutting is done. Ben turns on the faucet, splashes warm water over his chin and cheeks, and buries his face in a terry-cloth towel. Then he inspects the results, turning his face to the left, to the right, rubbing his fingertips over his stubble-free chin. I try to detect some change, but I see the same glossy face that he wore when we began this shaving lesson, maybe a bit cleaner beneath the nose, maybe a bit more self-satisfied.

"That'll do," he says. He thrusts out his bottom lip and nods.

As I step into the bathroom a couple of days later to take my evening shower, my bare feet detect something bulging under the throw rug. I lift the rug. Lying on the tile floor is a *Playboy* magazine, a voluptuous, half-naked woman pouting naughtily on the cover. I close the bathroom door, flip down the lid to the toilet and take a seat. It's an old issue, August 1990. Nothing terribly gynecological here. Airbrushed nudity.

Ben is the obvious owner, I reason. But how could he be so careless as to leave this behind? My first impulse is to confront him with it: Where did you get this? Or maybe I should subtly leave it lying face up on his desk and let him decide when and how to respond.

I open the bathroom door and start for his bedroom. But I stop myself midstride. What am I doing? Why humiliate him? Just what would I accuse him of doing, anyway? Being a healthy, evidently heterosexual fourteen-year-old boy?

I fold the *Playboy* under my arm. Ben is nowhere to be found. I decide to take the magazine to Cathy. She's sitting in the living room, reading a book.

"Look at this. I found it in the bathroom just now. Under the rug."

She stares at me, puzzled for a second. Then drops her jaw.

"Ben's," she sighs, taking the magazine in her hand as if she were accepting a summons to appear in court. "Where did he get this?" She's as much heartbroken as she is shocked. One more sign that her little boy is growing into a man.

"No doubt from one of his buddies," I say. "But, don't look so surprised. It's normal for a boy his age."

"How do I know what normal is?" she pleads. "I've never been a fourteen-year-old boy."

I tug at my ear. She has a point. "Look. He's going to be fifteen soon. I was stealing peeks at *Playboy* when I was Ben's age, even younger. He's not a child. I mean, *fifteen*. Biologically, he's old enough to be a father."

But this is not what a mother wants to hear.

"He won't be fifteen until March!" Cathy says, as if those five months were a very, very long time. "And even if he was eighteen, he shouldn't be looking at this stuff. The way women are portrayed is not only demeaning, but a complete fantasy. I don't want him growing up thinking every woman he meets should look like a *Playboy* centerfold."

I switch on a lamp and Cathy studies me.

"So what are you going to say to him?" she asks.

"Nothing. I think maybe it's best to look the other way sometimes."

"That's a cop-out," she says, and picks up the magazine again, gazing at the cover girl. "Look at her big ass," she says, tossing it onto the coffee table.

I tell her that I'm going to put the magazine back under the rug.

"He's done nothing wrong, why embarrass him? And I don't think this is really the right time to lecture him on how *Playboy* or *Penthouse* objectifies women. This is not a philosophical or political issue at the moment. This is hormones."

Cathy leans forward on the sofa, placing her fingertips together under her chin, as if in prayer. She shrugs and then nods.

"You better put it back before he comes home," she says. "You're right, he hasn't done anything wrong. But still . . ."

I return the *Playboy* to its hiding place, carefully placing it under the rug exactly as I found it. The magazine remains there for three days, with Cathy fretfully checking under the rug each time she uses the bathroom.

Nearly a week later, I tap on the open door of Ben's bedroom. He's sitting at his desk doing his homework. His back is to me, one hand supporting his head, the other holding a pencil. A small lamp is the only light in the room. It illuminates a paperback copy of *Romeo and Juliet* and a spiral notebook.

"Ben," I begin.

"Yep." He turns around in his wooden chair.

"You remember when you were in the seventh grade, and we talked about girls and—"

But he cuts me off in midthought.

"Dad, it's not like I just discovered girls." He tosses his head reflexively to throw the loose hair from his face. "And I'm not stupid. Nothing's going to happen."

I dig my hand in my pocket and rattle some change. I'm not sure how to respond. This wasn't in my script.

"But how can you be sure?" I sit down on the edge of his bed and lean toward him. "I mean, I know you're not stupid. But, you know, your mother, we *both* want to be certain that you . . . be careful, that's all I'm saying. You're still very young. Think about what you're doing, and think about what you're feeling. That sounds like a contradiction, I know, but . . . you don't want to break your mother's heart. Or mine."

He rolls the pencil over his knuckles and exhales, softly, self-consciously. "I know."

He's heard me out. I could recite statistics about teenage pregnancy. Or tell him about girls in my high school who got knocked up at age fourteen. Or hand him a pack of condoms. But I won't. I look into his eyes and he looks back, without a blink.

Ben comes home from school on a Friday afternoon, buoyant, energized. He decides to clean his bedroom and begins to sort through the debris that has collected on his desk and dresser—gum wrappers, pennies, chunks of candle wax, movie ticket stubs, overdue library books. The music of REM pounds from his stereo. An hour later I see him hauling an overflowing laundry basket down to the basement utility room, a sure sign that something's up.

In the evening, Cathy dishes out pasta with pesto sauce. At the dinner table, she brings up plans for the weekend.

"Maybe we can drive to Madison tomorrow for the day. The leaves are starting to turn colors."

"What time do you think we'd get home?" Ben asks.

"Dinner time?" I say, pouring Cathy and myself a glass of wine. "Or we could go out to eat somewhere."

He spears at his salad.

"I think I'm going out tomorrow night with Sarah. We'll probably go see a movie."

Cathy shoots me a look from across the table, a look first of happiness, then hurt. It's confirmed, she seems to say, resignedly. All is lost.

"Do you have a girlfriend?" Emma breaks in, her brown eyes wide. Not waiting for his answer, she repeats the question to her mother. "Does Ben have a girlfriend, Mommy?"

"Ben is going to a movie with a girl," Cathy states flatly, offering no additional information.

But to Emma, this is news enough. This is fodder for the kindergarten gossip mill. This juicy tidbit will score big points among her peers.

"What's her name?" Emma asks, and the inquest begins all over again.

Ben ignores his sister. He scrapes the last of the pesto from his plate with a fork and poses a question. "I was wondering if one of you could drive us to the movie theater. At least maybe one way. Chris is going too, with Karla. We can probably get one of their parents to pick us up."

I quickly volunteer. "Sure, I'll drive. Not a problem." I'm curious to meet his new friend.

We clear the plates from the table, stacking them on the kitchen counter, and Ben offers to wash. More unusual behavior. As he sloshes the dirty dishes into the sink, the telephone rings. I pick it up.

"Hi, is Ben there?" says an uncertain caller, a girl.

Ben wipes his hands on a dish towel and takes the phone into his bedroom to talk. He emerges a half hour later and walks into the pantry, searching for dessert.

"Can you take us to the seven o'clock show tomorrow night?" he asks me.

"What movie are you going to see?" I say, trying to act nonchalant.

"I think that new *Romeo and Juliet* movie. We're reading it now in English."

Ben's first date ever. A double date. To see *Romeo and Juliet*. Just a freshman.

On the first date I ever had with my first girlfriend, we went to a movie—*Romeo and Juliet*, the 1968 version made by Italian director Franco Zeffirelli. My father was the chauffeur. An amazing coincidence.

I was hesitant to ask him to drive us, afraid that he'd turn me down without an explanation, that he wouldn't allow me to go. But since I didn't have a driver's license, I really had no choice. I had to ask. Susie was counting on me.

I put the question to my father one evening after dinner in the presence of my mother, hoping that she would throw in her support. The two were sitting at the kitchen table having their after-dinner coffee. It was still light outside, the back door was open, the sun streaming cheerily through the window. My two brothers and my sister had scattered. The opportunity was right.

My father was surprisingly unconcerned about it. Sure he would drive, he said. He chuckled quietly and suggested that maybe I should buy flowers for my date. This made my mother smile.

On the drive to the theater, Susie and I sat in the back seat of the family car, a big, green Oldsmobile, biting our tongues. We were careful not to sit too close, not to touch. I was certain my father could see both of my hands in his rear-view mirror, even in the dark. I sat looking out the window, avoiding contact with my father's eyes in the mirror. He sat alone in the front seat and made small talk, asking Susie questions—"How are you doing in school? What kind of work is your father in?"—harmless questions, nothing humiliating at all.

KURT CHANDLER

We pulled up to the curb in front of the theater, and I opened the passenger door on Susie's side, not for Susie's sake, really, but for my father's. I was playing by his rules and I knew this was one of them.

My father picked us up at the curb at exactly the same spot two hours later. The date was uneventful. Susie and I hadn't kissed. I hadn't even put my arm around her. I was too afraid my father would read the guilt across my face after the show.

When I finally got my driver's license, the first date Susie and I went on was to watch a performance of the Broadway musical *Hair*. We had secretly bought tickets at the box office of the Palace Theater in Milwaukee, neither of us telling our parents. Susie's father came to the door when I rang her doorbell. I wore jeans and a blue Nehru jacket with a white turtleneck. I was trying to grow my first mustache, a wispy thing that Susie said tickled her lip when we kissed and made me look a little dangerous. Susie's father bowed slightly, pushed his glasses high on his nose, and looked me over from behind the screen door, but before he had a chance to say a word, Susie pushed past him out the door, laughing, and grabbed my arm. She was dressed in a white peasant shirt and tight bell-bottom jeans. She smelled of patchouli oil.

When we entered the theater, we were astonished that no one questioned our age. An usher inspected our tickets and escorted us to the very last row just as the house lights went down. The nudity came late in the play. The actors disrobed and stood as still as wax statues in the spotlights. But even from the rear of the theater, we had an unmistakable view of their bodies, their fuzzy shrubs of pubic hair, their breasts, their genitals.

We sat holding hands through the nude scene, our palms wet, looking straight ahead, not moving an inch, not saying a word, trying to act blasé, sophisticated. This was 1970, after all, and we were children of the Love Generation. Nothing should shock us anymore.

I took the long way home after the play and drove down Lincoln Memorial Drive along Lake Michigan. The moon shone on stormy whitecaps, but I didn't park. It was nearly curfew.

Ben does nothing special with his wardrobe for his first date, nothing that I would notice, at least. A pair of blue jeans, frayed at the hem, a black T-shirt with a logo of some band I'm not familiar with, and a flannel shirt, open at the front and unbuttoned at the sleeves. At the last minute, he decides to change his shoes. He trades a pair of black high-top Converse for red high-top Converse.

"Your fashion sense is impeccable," I joke as he sits in a chair, tying his laces. He shakes his head.

"Look at *you*," he dishes back. "You've probably had that old ragged blue shirt since I was a baby."

I look down at my button-down Oxford. "Before you were born, actually. Still fits. I don't like to throw away good clothes."

Cathy and Emma stand at the back door in the kitchen as Ben and I make our exit.

Ben lifts his sister from the floor and gives her a quick hug. "I'll see you in the morning, Emma."

"Are you coming home real late?" she asks.

"No," his mother answers for him, and Ben laughs. Cathy gives him a peck on the lips.

"Have a good time, Ben," she says. "And be nice." She flashes a generous smile. "I know you will."

I slip on a corduroy sport jacket and grab the keys to Cathy's Volvo from a ceramic bowl near the telephone. We'll take her car instead of my rust-bucket Subaru, I decide. Don't want to embarrass Ben. Or myself.

Ben sits in the front seat of the car with me and we drive first to his friend Chris's home. A tall, polite boy with black-framed glasses, Chris is wearing dark pants and a T-shirt. He greets me with a formal "Hello, Mr. Chandler," and I'm put in my place.

Chris directs me to the home of his date, Karla. The porch light shines in front of a large stone house with dark shutters, and Karla chugs down the sidewalk and opens the back door of the car. She is a short girl with shoulder-length hair, dressed in a striped T-shirt and black jeans. Chris welcomes her with a "Hi," and she returns the welcome.

Lastly, I'm directed to Sarah's house. The radio is tuned to Garrison Keillor's "A Prairie Home Companion." But as we turn onto Sarah's street, Ben lowers the volume so that Keillor's baritone is unintelligible. I slow the car, searching the street addresses.

"I think it's this one up here," Karla says, and I pull up to a white bungalow with black trim, nondescript except for two large maple trees in the yard. Instantly, a girl appears on the sidewalk.

Ben opens his passenger door and steps outside. He shuts the door, opens the rear door, and Sarah slides into the back seat. Ben slides in next to her and I'm left alone in the front, with four teenagers crushed together in the back.

When Cathy and I go out with another couple, it's not unusual for the men to take the front seat and the women to take the back. A double date once meant Cathy holding my hand or squeezing next to me in the front seat and our doubles squeezed next to each other in the back. No longer.

"Sarah, this is my dad," Ben instantly makes his introduction, and suddenly I'm self-conscious, wondering how I measure up in Ben's eye. I think to myself that maybe I should have changed my shirt. I turn to say hello over my shoulder and catch just a glimpse of Sarah as the dome light goes dark. Light brown hair, wire-rimmed glasses, taller than Ben, a pretty face, and the same sort of teenage uniform that each of the others wears.

It's a fifteen-minute drive to the theater. I catch comments from the back seat about high school and teachers and mutual friends. Karla is loud and boisterous, while Sarah waits to see how everyone else reacts before deciding when to laugh. I try to tune out the chatter and watch their body language in my rear-view mirror. As the street lights illuminate the foursome in the back seat, I see that no one is holding hands, no one has an arm around a shoulder.

I drove a taxi once for a living when I was in my mid-twenties. It was one of many dead-end jobs that inspired me to return to college. But I enjoyed the job for a while, especially working the graveyard shift. I got good at unobtrusively watching couples make out in the back seat of my cab. Sometimes a couple would ask me to dip the mirror and slide shut the plastic window that separated front from back. I complied, for the tip. But I could inconspicuously tilt the mirror at just the right angle where I'd see every move they made.

Now I'm checking out my *son's* moves. His posture is stiff, and when I turn a corner, he's careful to hold onto the hand grip above his head so as not to fall too close to Sarah's body.

Ben's eyes trap my gaze in the mirror and I quickly look away. I'm tempted to break into their conversation, to ask about their schoolwork, their special interests, to ask about their families, their parents, their own fathers. But I focus on the highway, content to play the silent chauffeur. This is their time.

I roll up to the curb at the theater. A crowd of people rushes past the car and through the glass door under the white marquee, which has orange lights swirling around the names of literature's most famous couple. The passengers charge out. "Thank you, Mr. Chandler," they sing together. "Thank you, Mr. Chandler," repeats Ben, just for the effect. And they walk away laughing and grinning, joking about things I already know and things I never will.

Two weeks pass. I come home late in the evening after having a beer with a friend. The house is dark except for a light over the kitchen sink. Emma is asleep, and Cathy is reading upstairs. Ben's bedroom door is shut, but I hear him talking on the phone. His voice is low, without humor.

Through the bedroom door, I hear him sign off by saying, "Sorry about all this."

I hang my jacket in the closet, and a minute later, Ben opens the door of his room. He leans against the doorjamb in the dark. Something is on his mind. I say hello and wait for his reply.

"I just broke up with Sarah," he says, sadly but certainly.

I let the words settle.

"Why? What happened?" I raise my eyebrows.

"Nothing really happened," Ben says, his hands in his back pockets. "I was thinking about it over the weekend, and I don't know, I decided I didn't want to go out with anyone right now. I guess I think I'm too young."

I don't speak. I'm astonished, not only by the news, but by Ben's frankness and by his insight. This is a concession that not every teenage boy would make to his father.

I don't have a lot of words for him. I believe he is wise beyond his years, that his self-awareness is immense. But I can only put my feelings into words that a father would say.

"That's a very mature decision to make. If that's how you feel, then you should trust your feelings. You're the one who knows best."

I say no more. I step closer, squeeze his arm, muss up his hair, and say good night.

The Family Home

My mother calls in a fit of panic.

"There's a squirrel in my basement!" she says, her voice raised an octave. "It must have fallen down the chimney and found its way in through the furnace."

She saw the furry thing scurry across the basement floor while she was sorting laundry. She fled upstairs, slamming the door behind her. Then she called her next-door neighbor and asked him to come open a window in her basement, in hope that the animal would just please *leave*.

"I'm sure I won't get any sleep tonight," she tells me. She has visions of a rabid rodent entering the heating ducts somehow, squeezing through the heat register in her bedroom and attacking her in bed.

But she calls back in the evening, sounding much calmer. She has not heard a thing beneath her floorboards for hours now, so she's fairly confident the squirrel has beaten a hasty exit out the open window. To play it safe, though, her neighbor has placed a cage-trap in the basement to capture the poor beast should it still be lurking in a dark corner somewhere.

"It's one thing after another," she says of life in general.

It's early fall, and my mother is preparing to move. She has sold her home of thirty-eight years, the family home. The buyers are a young couple with two young children, a family configuration that greatly pleases Mom. The young family will move in, and my mother will begin a new episode in her life. Just what that episode will be is unclear at this point. But to ease her separation anxiety, her real estate agent has assured her that the buyers will let her visit her soon-to-be-former home whenever she wants.

It has been more than seven years since my father died, and it has taken my mother all those years to prepare for the day when she will leave behind forever The House That Kent Built. The solid-oak cabinets in the kitchen, custom-made with my mother's height in mind; the big bay window, with a window seat facing out to the parklike backyard; the china cabinet in the dining room, with its finely mitered woodwork, holding porcelain plates and crystal that sparkles through the glass doors; the bathroom vanity, painted ivory and gilded to give the room a regal touch—all were made by my father's hand, painstaking projects, crafted to perfection.

The house was a labor of love for my parents. They were both in their late twenties when they bought it. It was the first (and only) house they owned. They decided to build in the rural suburb of New Berlin. The name itself conveyed a promise of new opportunities, new beginnings, particularly to my father, whose ancestry was German. My father had just started his carpentry business. My mother was pregnant with my sister, the third child of four.

The house was not finished when they moved in. The walls needed paint. The floors were bare wood. The basement was empty and damp. The outside brickwork was only halfway completed. There was no grass, there were no trees or bushes or landscaping of any sort, just mounds of black dirt on a half-acre lot. But the following summer, with the help of good friends and relatives, my parents made the house a home for their growing family, and through the years, they never stopped working on it.

It was a modest house, a single-story ranch with an attached two-car garage; three bedrooms; a bath and a half; a small dining room for birthdays, holiday dinners, and games of Monopoly; and a long hallway for foot races between my brother and me. Wide picture windows in the living room and dining room brought in sunlight from the east and west. Because of the way the lots in the subdivision were graded, the house sat in what amounted to a flood plain. This caused endless frustration for my parents, but it was okay with me. When it rained, the drainage creek that bordered the backyard swelled, sometimes spilling into our basement, providing my friends and me with a fine opportunity to launch boats that we had constructed out of scrap lumber. In the winter, my father joined forces with Mother Nature and flooded the backyard with a hose to make an ice rink for the kids.

Kent and Rose Chandler had four children; a child was born every three years, beginning with me in 1953 and ending in 1962. My brother Steven and I shared a bedroom, and a bunk bed was added years later when Gregory, the fourth child, came along. Kathleen, the only girl, had a room of her own.

My parents' marital roles were typical of the times: My mother chose the wallpaper and carpeting and paint colors and floor tile. She planted the flower beds: zinnias, bleeding hearts, clematis, and marigolds. She cultivated the vegetable garden: green beans, snap peas, sweet corn, and lettuce. And she tended to the children: meals, laundry, shopping, and cleaning. My father the carpenter was in charge of repairs and renovation, of course. He transformed half of the basement into a recreation room, enclosing the ceiling with soundproof tiles, covering the cinder-block walls with knotty pine and large murals of mountainscapes, designing a wet bar in a corner. He poured the cement for the driveway and for a backyard patio. He raised the walls of a storage shed near the garage, big enough to hold instruments both of work and of pleasure: shovels, rakes, and a lawnmower as well as a volleyball net and a fleet of bicycles. He put up a basketball hoop and fashioned storm windows for the sliding glass doors. He hauled wheelbarrows of topsoil from one end of the lot to the other, laying sod, stacking flagstone along the perimeter of the garden, and planting junipers, bridal wreaths, sunburst locust, silver-leaf maples, blue spruce, and privet hedges. And more than two decades after signing the mortgage contract, he installed a huge, round, aboveground swimming pool in the backyard, at long last allowing himself some pastime.

There are memories of my father in every square inch of that house, on every square foot of that yard, in everything my mother touches, through every door she opens. For a long time, the deep, lingering memories immobilized my mother. She teetered on the brink of indecision for years. On one day she would lean toward making a clean break and getting on with her life, then the next day she'd swing the other way and vow to remain in the house forever. "They'll have to carry me out of here in a box," she would announce, echoing the stubborn sentiments of her husband.

Her uncertainty drove her children wild. "You're living in a monument," I would say, frustrated with her reluctance, "a monument to Dad. It's time to move on." But move on to what? She didn't know, and no one could tell her.

Inevitably, each sibling came to the conclusion that there was no sense trying to persuade her. Our advice was useless. Mom had to make up her mind on her own time. And eventually she did.

The offer on the sale of her house was a good one. She will invest her profits and, combined with her monthly Social Security checks, have enough money to live on for years to come. It won't be an extravagant lifestyle; she will live on a fixed income, yet comfortably—able to afford day trips and dinners with friends and vacations to southern California to visit her younger sister. She has found a two-bedroom apartment in a large complex not far from her home, but it's a temporary move. She knows she will not be happy there for long. There are no flower beds, and most disappointingly, there are few residents who are her age; most are much younger.

Last weekend, I wondered out loud if Cathy and I should buy a duplex with her and share living space.

"It would be easier on my mother if she had someone nearby all the time," I reasoned.

"Ben and Emma would love having Grandma around," Cathy said. "And I wouldn't mind, I suppose, but what about you? I don't think you could handle it. I don't know if you would want to."

"Maybe it's guilt talking," I said, "guilt of the first-born son."

I was beginning to feel caught in a generational role reversal, where children become parents to their own parents, and I was hesitant to take on that role—hesitant and a little afraid of the consequences. It was one thing having two children depend on me for their daily minimum requirements, but living next door to my mother . . . I'm not that patient a man. I will keep an eye on her health, help her with her finances, and see that she is comfortable in her golden years. But I can't provide the companionship that she lost when my father died. As much as I love her, we seem to get along best when there's some distance separating us, even if it's only a couple of miles.

"What she really needs," Cathy said, "are neighbors who are her own age, a community of her generation."

"I think you're right. She'll be fine, for now. We'll see what comes later."

On a Sunday, the entire Chandler clan gathers at the family home. Today, in an all-day scramble, we will pack up the homestead and celebrate my mother's upcoming move.

Ben and I decide to drive to my mother's early to get a head start on the work. I pull into the driveway and see that the garage door is open. The garage is jammed with cardboard boxes and stacks of yellowed newspaper and old tires leaning against a wall and piles and piles of household junk.

"It's going to be a long day," I say to Ben, as we climb out of the car.

We walk around the house to the back door, a habit instilled years ago by my mother to keep her kids from tracking mud on her living room carpet. When we enter, I see that all the house lights have been turned up bright even though it's not yet noon.

"Hello, Ben," my mother says as she slides back her kitchen chair. "Give me a hug." She smiles. "I need my hugs." She reaches up to give her oldest grandchild her customary squeeze around his shoulders. Ben smiles and takes a cracker from a box on the table.

"How are you doing, Mom?" I say, and I bend to give her a hug.

"I'm fine, a little tired from all this packing, but okay."

Dressed in a T-shirt with turquoise seahorses on the front, she looks younger than her sixty-six years. Her black hair is laced with gray, rheumatoid arthritis has slowed her down, but she's still energetic, still adventurous, daring at times. She will gladly ride a roller coaster with her grandkids at the state fair midway, or dive into a lake from the side of a motorboat on a muggy August day.

Ben sits down at the table. I lean against the kitchen counter and roll up the sleeves of my blue-jean shirt, anxious to get to work, unlike Ben. But my mother is chatty, with no one to talk to during her days. She grew up in a large Italian family, one of a throng of cousins all about the same age who saw each other routinely at family weddings, summer picnics, and Sunday afternoon dinners. She's a social creature by nature, always the one leading the conversation during the meal.

My mother also has a knack for remembering a person's first name. It's more than a knack, really, it's an obsession. She's on a first-name basis with just about everyone she's ever met. Once she commits a name to memory, that person becomes a dear friend for life. Complete strangers become family. Her car mechanic is Joe. The dental assistant is Lucy. The guy who came in to steam-clean her carpet last Tuesday is Fred. The Avon Lady from 1987 is still Betty. And she will drop the names in conversations with people who never *have* and never *will* met these newfound friends of hers. "You know, Fred was telling me his daughter Sally is a sophomore at Tosa East High School. Do you know her, Ben?" It's the way she is, a way that makes me crazy sometimes. When I stop to think about it, though, it's how we all should live. If we all remained on a first-name basis with everyone we'd ever met, the world would be a much friendlier place.

"Kurt, help yourself to a cup of coffee," my mother says. "Ben, would you like some juice?" She opens the refrigerator while I take a coffee mug from the cupboard.

"So how's school going, Ben?" she asks.

"Good. We've been doing ceramics in my art class. It's a lot of fun."

"I was thinking of signing up for a watercolor class through some adult education program I heard about," she says. "I've always wanted to paint."

"Well then you should, Mom, you really should," I say.

Ben takes another handful of crackers. "And next week," he says, "I'm going to trying out for the golf team. I don't know if I'll make it, though. There's a lot of competition."

"You know there might be some golf clubs in the shed," she says. "Belonged to your grandfather. Have you looked out there?"

"I've got a set of clubs," he says.

"Oh, that's right. I've forgotten." She stands, shifting her attention to two stained-glass ornaments hanging in the bay window.

"Ben, honey, would you help me with these? You're tall enough, could you take these down for me? I remember when Kent first put in this window. The kitchen seemed so much bigger and brighter. I had to hang curtains right away."

Ben kneels on the window seat and takes a stained-glass bird from a hook. He hands it to his grandmother and she begins to wrap it in newspaper. Two or three cardboard boxes are stacked on the kitchen floor.

"I'm excited about moving," says my mother. "I'm ready to go, I really am. This place is just too much for me. I can't keep up with the yard work and everything else. I'm ready to move."

"It's going to be a big change, but I think it'll be good for you," I say. "It might take a while to adjust, but you'll be just fine. It's a new start."

"You know," she says, "today will be the last time we'll all be together in this house."

"You'll just have to invite us over to your new place," I say.

I pace the floor, walking through the kitchen doorway, down the hall, back into the living room, into the dining room, glancing through the window to the wide backyard. I step back into the kitchen and I see myself as a boy, my homework spread on the kitchen table in the late afternoon, my mother standing at the white stove, stirring a wooden spoon in a pan, singing to herself as she cooks—"*Que sera, sera . . . Whatever will be, will be . . .*"—her hair jet black and wavy from the home perms she would give herself, her voice lilting and sweet.

I will miss this house, this yard, miss coming down the street that has always led me here, home.

"Well, Ben," I say, clapping my hands and chasing away the memories, "let's get to it."

Our first task takes us to the basement rec room. Several ceiling tiles have come loose and have fallen over the past few years. Fortunately, my father kept an extra carton of tiles on hand.

"It looks like we'll have to replace about four or five," I say, counting the white square tiles. "A couple more over here have water stains from a leaky pipe. We'll have to rip these out, too."

I have a small can of adhesive, a putty knife, and a utility blade for the work.

"See if you can find a screwdriver, and a tape measure or ruler on the workbench," I say to Ben, sending him running, and suddenly I sound like my father, ordering one of his kids to fetch one thing or another as he plunged into his latest project. An unbroken devotion to work was my father's burden. No matter how large or small the job, he was always preoccupied with the project. Seldom would a weekend pass when he wouldn't recruit one of his sons—usually me, the oldest—to help him replace a cracked window or hang a set of shelves in the garage, instructing me to lug the belt sander out of his truck or get a pair of pliers out of his toolbox. To my father, a Saturday project was a hands-on lesson in responsibility. To a teenager, it had all the appearances of punishment.

Ben returns with two screwdrivers. "I couldn't find a ruler," he says.

"That's okay, we'll make do."

I pry open the can of adhesive and pass it to Ben. I unfold a small aluminum ladder and size up a gap in the ceiling. The gap exposes gray sheetrock underneath.

"We'll have to cut off this tab on the side of the tile to make it fit," I say. I mark the tile with a pencil, guessing the distance to cut. "Then we'll dab a little glue on the corners and stick it to the sheetrock. Simple as that."

I step down from the ladder and lay the tile on top of the bar. Ben watches as I pare down the side of the tile with the utility blade.

"I remember helping my father put this ceiling up," I say. "Seemed like it took forever. I used to spend a lot of time down here. When I was a teenager, all three boys shared one bedroom, and so this became my hangout. I listened to music down here. Had stereo speakers in the corners. Your grandma and grandpa had parties in this room, too, costume parties on Halloween, New Year's Eve. My brother Steve and I used to sneak down the stairs and watch all their friends drink and act goofy, everyone dancing the jitterbug."

I think about one of the last times I saw my father in this house. It was late fall and the entire family had gathered for a Sunday dinner. The cancer had gone to my father's brain, and he had difficulty keeping his balance. His eyesight and hearing had begun to deteriorate. He couldn't speak louder than a whisper.

But despite his illness, he continued to drive. Just months before the cancer was found, he had bought a baby blue Cadillac Coupe De Ville. He would cruise the country roads, one hand on the big steering wheel, the other holding a cigar, flicking the ashes out of the wing window.

During dinner one evening, he and I got into an argument. I was angry that he was still working so much. He seemed to be denying that he was even ill. My mother was so afraid of upsetting him that she would take the telephone outside to the patio and out of his earshot whenever she called the oncologist.

"You can't just go on with your life as if nothing's wrong," I shouted at him, and everyone at the table turned silent. "You've got to slow down, think about what you're going to do, make some . . . preparations."

And for the first time that I could remember, my father couldn't respond. There was no force to be released, no words, no voice, no sound at all. He stood from the table, gave me a long and bitter look, and walked outside.

I followed, minutes later, and found him standing in the driveway, rattling his car keys in his hand.

"What are you doing? Where are you going?" I asked.

He turned, staggered a bit, and in a dusty, barely audible voice said, "I'm taking the Caddie for a drive." He paused for a second, then looked up at me with an expression I had never seen before. Was it embarrassment? Defiance? Fear? Did he want me to come?

"Be careful," was the only reply I could give him. And off he went, alone, on one last drive . . .

"I remember Grandpa teaching me how to play pool down here," Ben says as I step up on the ladder. "He sat me on the end of the table and lined up all the balls on the other end, and I tried to knock them all into the pockets."

"I remember that," I say.

Ben dips the putty knife in the pasty adhesive.

"Spread a little of that goo in the middle of this tile."

"And I remember that model train he set up for me down here," Ben continues.

"I played with that train when I was a kid. All of us kids did." I take the tile from Ben and try to wedge it into place. "Well, it doesn't seem to fit. Damn. Why won't it fit?"

"You're not getting it right," I hear my father's voice in the corner of my mind. "The tile is too large." He takes the tile in one hand and holds a utility blade in the other. Bracing the tile, he scores it once, then in the second pass shaves off another half inch, slicing the tile precisely and evenly.

"Now turn it this way," he says, rotating the tile with his large hands. "Slide it under the tab on this side, and push it into place. Like this."

"There," I say to Ben, sliding it under the tab and pushing it into place. "Perfect fit. No gaps, nice and tight. Nothing to it. Let's put up another one."

We repeat the process several times, dragging the step ladder across the floor, trimming, gluing, each tile going up quicker than the last. When the final tile is set into place, I fold the ladder and collect the tools. We stand side by side, smudges of glue on our hands and faces, heads tilted back as we inspect our work. The ceiling is once again whole, solid white, no gaps.

"Good job, Ben."

"Good job, Dad," he returns the compliment. And as we turn to climb the stairs, one of the tiles falls free from the ceiling and plops onto the basement floor.

I shake my head and we hoot at each other.

"What happened?" my mother calls down from the kitchen, and I'm fourteen years old again, guiltily trying to hide my stupid blunder from my parents.

* * *

The rest of the Chandler family arrives in installments. As usual, everyone dives right into the cleanup project, heeding the command of our cursed work ethic. The backyard barbecue will wait until later.

Steve backs his pickup truck up the driveway, Greg waving him to the edge of the open garage. It's not hard to see that Greg, Steve, and I are brothers. We all have dark hair, brown eyes, and broad cheeks. We're about the same height. Like me, Greg wears a beard, but without a trace of gray (he's still young, not yet forty). Steve is muscular, clean shaven. His hair is clipped short, as thick as it was when he was a kid.

"Why don't we load all this crap into the truck and haul it to the dump?" Greg suggests dryly, looking around at the hodge-podge. "That would simplify things."

"Oh no you don't." Our mother steps into the garage. She swats Greg across the chest with the back of her hand. "I want all you kids to go through these odds and ends. Divvy up anything you might want. The rest can be thrown away or given away to charity." She picks up a *National Geographic* with a caption about the USSR on the cover. "Ben, do you want any of these?"

Ben shakes his head.

"I sold a lot of things at my rummage sale last week," my mother says, "garden hoses, yard tools, the lawnmower, things I'll never need again. I gave my wedding dress to the Goodwill."

"You gave away your wedding dress?" Greg says.

"Why not? It was sitting in a box, turning yellow. I'll be glad to get rid of the rest of this stuff."

But this *stuff*—the highball glasses no longer used, the coffee percolator that no longer works, the 78-rpm records, the polyester neckties—this stuff embodies a lifetime of memories for her. All month long, she has been carefully clearing the last of the relics from the shadows of her closets, hauling to the garage things that she could not part with until now.

"I can't believe it, look at these." Steve holds out two plastic hoola hoops.

I can see the two of us as boys, spinning them around our waists—mine green, Steve's orange—shimmying as if we'd been struck by epilepsy, counting the seconds ("nine one-thousand, ten one-thousand") that each of us could keep his hoop twisting before it lost its centrifugal force and dropped to his feet.

"Take them," I say to Steve. "Give them to your boys."

"Are you kidding, they'd be bored in two minutes," and he tosses them onto a pile destined for the trashman.

We fan out, working like army ants, beating paths from the basement, through the bedrooms, up and down a ladder to the attic, into the kitchen, out to the patio, through the garage and down to the end of the driveway, where a trash pile is forming for the Monday morning garbage truck. Ben hangs out in the garage with his cousins Nick and Jake, the sons of Steve and his wife, Sue. They poke around in plastic crates and cardboard boxes, more curious than helpful.

"Help me with this, would you, Ben?" I say.

We carry out the steel-tube frame of a hammock that my siblings and I bought one year as a Father's Day gift; the hammock became an unused lawn ornament.

Nick, three years younger than Ben, has found a bowling ball in a black vinyl carrying case.

"Can I have this?" he asks, but his father says no.

"We already have more things than we know what to do with," Steve says.

Nevertheless, Nick and Ben decide they have to give the bowling ball a try. They take the ball onto the patio, where they line up plastic flower pots and empty soda cans from the recycling bin as bowling pins.

"Yeah, all right!" says Ben as he sends the substitute pins flying.

Three look-alike girls suddenly run into the garage, Emma and her cousins Samantha and Andrea, brown eyes wide with mischief. Sam and Andi are twins, a year younger than Emma, the daughters of my sister and her husband, Dale.

"Where's Jake?" whispers Emma, and Jake leaps out from under a folding table and roars, sending the girls screaming across the patio and into the backyard.

Steve and Dale tackle the workbench. They load any salvageable lumber into the back of Steve's pickup, but most of what they find is junk—dried paintbrushes, rusty tools, and coffee cans filled with finishing nails, lag bolts, and fragments of hardware no one can identify.

Steve fishes something from a drawer and lobs it my way. It's a Pinewood Derby car, made when I was a Cub Scout. The model car was one of the first projects I worked on with my father. He did most of the work, I'm sure—fathers can't resist commandeering a Cub Scout project; it satisfies some unwritten manhood requirement and provides them with a good excuse to show their offspring how to use tools. By demonstration, he taught me how to carve down the corners of the wooden block with his pocket knife, thin and razor sharp; how to sand the soft, white pine so it was perfectly smooth and rounded, front and back; how to apply the glossy enamel paint, blue and gold. I added decals of fire bolts on the sides, and my father glued a strip of clear plastic over the cockpit as a bubble-top windshield. I don't remember winning the race, but that was never the point.

"Maybe I'll hold on to this," I say and walk out to the driveway and drop the model into the backseat of my car.

Greg and his longtime girlfriend, Ann, rummage through the storage shed, hauling out a bag of rusty golf clubs, empty paint cans, and loose bicycle parts.

"Hey, who wants this?" Greg lifts a small outboard motor, used by our father on fishing trips.

"Oh, man, not me," I say.

I think about the times my father took me fishing. Sitting in a small aluminum boat in the cold mist of some northern lake, those Saturday mornings bordered on drudgery. From a tackle box, my father would choose a brightly colored lure for each of us. "Pink, they like pink this time of the day," he'd declare. He would fix the lure to my line, then instruct me where to cast.

"Left," he would whisper, so as not to spook the phantom walleye or muskellunge, and I'd cast to the left and sit, silently, perfectly inert, my back arched and aching, watching my red-and-white bobber drift listlessly on the water's surface. After what seemed like hours without a single bite, my father would fire up the Evinrude and race to another part of the lake. "This is the spot," he would say, cutting the engine in a deserted cove, confident that the lake's entire fish population had conspiratorially collected in the shallows now beneath our stealthy boat. And then he'd laugh at himself and attach a new lure to my line. "Yellow. They like yellow this time of the day."

My brother-in-law, Dale, makes a play for the outboard. "I'll take it if no one else wants it."

No one does.

"It's all yours, Dale," I say. "Happy fishing."

I take a break and walk into the house for a beer. In the kitchen, my mother and her daughters-in-law, Cathy and Sue, are preparing dinner: hamburgers and brats, potato salad, and end-of-the-season sweet corn. Meanwhile, my sister empties a closet in what used to be her bedroom. Still on hangers are clothes she wore more than a dozen years ago.

"I remember this dress," Kathleen says, amazed to see the red shift again. She holds it up and strolls around the bedroom. "I think I wore this to a job interview. I didn't get the job." She throws the dress onto a heap of Goodwill giveaways.

I take my Heineken into the living room and sit in a cushioned rocking chair. This was my father's chair. It's still hard to sit in it without expecting to hear him boom in his best Archie Bunker voice: "You're in my chair. Up. *Up.*" Once it was petty and annoying to me, my father's padded throne; today, it's a funny recollection.

When I was a boy, my father and I watched war movies and Westerns together here in the living room, he in his overstuffed chair, a long-necked bottle of Schlitz at his side, me stretched out on the carpet, a bag of potato chips passing between us. I looked forward to the experience, mostly because it was something to do with Dad. Most exciting were the war movies—*Bridge on the River Kwai*, *The Longest Day*, *Pork Chop Hill.*

"Get those Krauts!" my father would bellow at the TV set, as if we were watching the Packers play the Bears. And I would cheer as the GIs rushed a Nazi machine-gun nest behind the front lines. Guns blazed, a grenade was tossed, soldiers fell. No blood, no gore, no pain. War was sanitized and glorified for our viewing pleasure.

My father was not a veteran. He was too young to serve in World War II, and when Korea came along, a head injury from a car crash rendered him medically ineligible for duty. Though never stated in conversation, I learned something about my father by watching TV with him. These war movies were an expression of his beliefs, an expression of his view of the world, of duty, service, heroism, manhood, America, of values that shaped his identity, values that defined a generation of Americans—values that my generation would later question.

With Vietnam, the color images of the TV news reports were dangerously more vivid than the black-and-white Hollywood depictions of past wars. Live broadcasts of body bags in helicopters didn't jibe with the Late Show features of idols Gary Cooper and John Wayne. The contrast was hard for a young teenager to reconcile. Suddenly there was nothing entertaining about combat, nothing honorable about war, nothing necessary about the violence. I stopped watching war movies with my father, and as I turned the corner into adolescence, our opinions began to diverge.

Like my father, I never served in the military. When I turned eighteen and became eligible for the draft, a high lottery number spared me from military service. But unlike my father, I was ready to do anything to avoid it.

The pile at the end of the driveway grows into a mountain of debris as the house is slowly emptied. Throughout the afternoon, we all stash personal mementos in the trunks of our cars, items retrieved as if from a lost-and-found—clothes and books and toys and knickknacks, small treasures that no one else would value, things that once could be identified as part of a family but now are just random souvenirs. Alas, no one has uncovered my collection of baseball cards, missing now for twenty-five years and probably worth enough money to pay for Ben's first year of college and a vacation to Greece. But I salvage a couple of baseball bats for Ben; a quartz geode for Emma's rock collection; a set of five beer steins, the brand name Schlitz embossed in red on each glass; my high school team jacket; and an electric drill of my father's, its handle worn smooth by his grip.

By the middle of the afternoon, the intrigue of digging through our pasts begins to wear off. Patience is growing thin and each of us falls silent as we work, at once glum and testy. We begin to snap at each other, tired and angry; angry at our mother for her years of delaying, angry at our father for his absence, angry at each other for no reason at all.

"You're not saving that worthless piece of shit, are you?" I taunt my brother Greg. He's holding a huge table lamp with a snow-cone-shaped shade.

"What do you care?" he snarls back. "It's my worthless piece of shit, not yours."

The reality of the task is sinking in: We are preparing the family home for a new family, a family of strangers. It's hard to imagine, kids we've never met running sticky fingers along the walls of the dining room, an unknown couple making love in our parents' bedroom. Though we don't express it in words, this is a difficult adjustment for all of us, a tough assignment, disassembling the house we grew up in. The day begins to feel less like a backyard picnic than a funeral.

The sun begins to sink over Hollywood Hill behind the house. Long green shadows stretch across the backyard lawn from the fat trunks of a row of pine trees. My mother opens the screen door, looks into the sun, and walks onto the patio. She summons us to the backyard to stand for a portrait.

"Come on, everybody," she calls, sweeping her grandchildren onto the back lawn. "It's getting late. Let's take a picture before dinner. We need one more family picture here."

Grudgingly, we stop our work and troop into the backyard.

I retrieve my camera and tripod from my car and walk across the grass. The afternoon has been controlled chaos, all of us darting about in separate directions, moving on our own course, on our own mission. Now we fold in, circle around, tie together in the backyard as a group, as one unit.

"Okay, let's all stand together next to that tree," I say, motioning everyone into place. "Right here, near the big pine tree."

The backyard has been the locus of this family. It was many things to us—ice-skating rink, baseball diamond, army battlefield, and backdrop for our high school prom photos, wedding pictures, baby pictures. It was also a cool sanctuary when a person needed to be alone. It will be the hardest thing to give up. I remember helping plant that very pine tree when I was seven or eight. The sapling was a foot and a half tall, no more. Long, soft needles brushed against my arm as I tamped the black earth over its roots. Now it shoots thirty feet into the air.

I look into the viewfinder and focus the lens.

"Tallest people in the back," I say, directing the group. "Kathleen, that is not you, sorry. Stand in front of Dale. And the three girls, line up with Jake. Ben, you're blocking a view of your mother's lovely face."

The bitterness begins to leave us. With the lens aimed at us, we're now forced to smile. How can we be framed in a Kodachrome pose as a brooding gang of reprobates, with deep creases in our foreheads and scowls across our lips? We have no choice but to lighten up. We wait for a cloud to pass overhead, and as the setting sun breaks through, laughter breaks on our faces, sisters and brothers and cousins and mothers and daughters and nieces and aunts and uncles and fathers and sons, shoulder to shoulder, celebration returning to our day.

"Okay, let's fire one off." I step back. "Everybody ready?"

We smile for the camera, for each other, for the family.

A week later, I take one last walk through the house. The moving van will arrive the next morning for the furniture, and my mother will make a new home.

I go from room to room, closet to closet, with a screwdriver and pliers in my hands, still disassembling, removing anything that was overlooked. I take down a set of wind chimes on the patio, a hanging basket of dried flowers in the bathroom, my father's tie rack in a bedroom closet.

I stack a couple of more souvenirs at the front door before I step out: the tie rack, my father's tackle box. As I gaze around the living room, I take one last look inside the stereo console. This long piece of cherry-wood furniture was once my parents' pride and joy. A receiver and phonograph, with booming speakers built into each end, the big Magnavox, "the stereo," as it was simply known, brought wonderful music into our home for years and years, from my parents' scratchy 78s of Benny Goodman and Nat King Cole, Perry Como and Patti Page, to

89

my mother's prized soundtracks of *Camelot* and *The Sound of Music*, from the kids' *Mary Poppins*, to my first playing of *Sgt. Pepper's Lonely Hearts Club Band.*

Inside the cabinet, I find a few old records, 45s that once belonged to me—a couple of singles by the Beatles, an easily forgotten hit called "Judy in Disguise (With Glasses)," and a song with a catchy melody that will play on my mind for the rest of the afternoon: "Those Were the Days."

Anger and Reconciliation

Emma yawns as I usher her through the door of the bathroom, following behind as she trudges along in her stocking feet. In keeping with the division of labor in our home, I am the parent responsible in the mornings for helping her wash her sweet face, brush her tiny teeth, and comb her shiny hair. Cathy, meanwhile, lays out Emma's school clothes and packs her lunchbox each day. Ben, for the most part, is responsible for himself.

It's a Friday, a glorious Wisconsin autumn day, with a promising weekend in the forecast. Outside the window, red and gold leaves sparkle as they cascade to the ground. Inside, spirits are high as we prepare for the day.

But a booby trap lies on the bathroom floor in the form of a damp bath towel, property of Ben.

"This again," I mumble as Emma spits her toothpaste down the drain. A green towel is heaped in a corner next to the toilet, the same green towel that had occupied the same corner the day before until I hung it on the rack. I snatch it from the floor, sweep past Emma, and march into the living room. Ben slouches on the sofa reading the paper, his shoes on the coffee table.

I dangle the towel in the air.

"Ben. What is this?"

He keeps on reading, then glances up absently from the sports page.

"Let me guess. A towel?"

It's a typical smart-ass response from a typical smart-ass fourteen-year-old. And normally I'd let it slide, or come back with a smart-ass response of my own. After all, I take much of the blame (or credit) for instilling in Ben an appreciation of the art of sarcasm. But he levels his remark at me with a look of such disdain—a steel-piercing glower that I see more and more as he grows older, a look of such pure distaste for everything I represent—that I lose it. I blow up.

"God*damn* it, Ben." My circle of vision suddenly caves in. I can see no light, no color, no detail. Only the smug scowl of Ben's face.

And it becomes my target.

I lunge for him. I rip the newspaper from his hands and hook him around the head with my left arm, knocking him off balance and pinning him in a headlock, pushing his smug little face into the cushions.

He goes down without resistance, taken aback at the swiftness and force of my rage. But then he panics.

"Don't touch me! Don't touch me! Get your hands off of me!" he screams, spitting into the cushion, frantically trying to break free.

And in seconds, it's over. I release my grip and push away, straightening myself, lingering over him.

Ben springs to his feet and out of my reach. His ears are blood red. His T-shirt is hiked halfway up his back. His glasses lie on the carpet under the table.

"Now get the hell to school," I hear myself say in one final burst. Ben looks at me for a long second, his face a reflection of shock and utter, desperate hurt.

Cathy rushes into the room. "What happened, what's going on?" she asks, a witness only to the aftermath.

Emma watches, speechless and frightened, hiding behind her mother.

"I'm out of here," mutters Ben, waving his mother off. Eyes damp and downcast, he grabs his backpack and stomps out the front door, not bothering to retrieve his glasses, his hair shooting wildly in all directions. He slams the screen door, leaps down the porch steps, and runs down the sidewalk.

I hover in the middle of the living room, dizzy now, the adrenaline drained from me. And across the room, in the hallway mirror, I catch a glimpse of my reflection. Face sullen, brow furrowed, jaw tight, eyes narrow and manic. I recognize the face. It's my father's face, the same face that raged at me so many times, so many years ago.

Damn.

My father.

Damn. Damn. *Damn.*

I push past Cathy without a word, storm out the back door and onto the patio. I shiver in the warm morning sunlight. The rage has left me, but I'm rocked by a landslide of other emotions. Shame, humiliation, sorrow, fear.

This is awful, I think. What did I do? What happened? Oh shit. This is just awful.

My father was a disciplinarian. His rules of order were rigid and direct. There was never any doubt that in his house, disobedience would be met with consequences. The form of discipline ranged, depending, of course, on the infraction that had been committed. Punishment was predictable, meted out quid pro quo. For the act of pummeling my younger brother I would be banished to my bedroom for the evening. For leaving my bike out in the rain, my bike would remain in the garage for a full week. For stealing a candy bar from the five-and-dime, no allowance for a month. For skipping school: "You're grounded until I say so."

One of the worst offenses that could be committed was talking back. "I don't want to hear any more lip out of you" was a common refrain of my father's. If the lip ceased to be stilled, the punishment could turn corporal—a spanking, or a "lickin'," as it was grimly referred to.

Talking back to my mother, in particular, would bring swift and decisive action—a flurry of smacks to the seat of the pants from my father's open hand. His hands were large, muscular, the working hands of a carpenter. Sometimes a quick smack to the back of the head would remedy a wisecrack. Sometimes he threatened with his belt, unfastening the silver buckle and slowly slipping it out of the loops until the offender apologized or agreed to amend his mischievous ways or fled screaming into the night. But the belt was just intimidation, never applied. Spankings were dispensed with an open palm, no fist, no paddle. But still throbbingly painful.

Yet it wasn't the punishment itself that was most feared. Even the sting of a lickin' would wear off eventually. No, it was my father's hair-trigger temper that planted fear and dread into the hearts of my siblings and me. It stayed there for years, until we were past adolescence and out of his house, out of his reach. Sometimes the most seemingly harmless remark—usually laced with sarcasm—would set him off. He would erupt in a loud roar, shouting us into silence, into acquiescence. I can see him driving the car, my mother in the front seat, children in the back. One of us kids would do something that would get under his skin—spit out the window or open the rear door while we were moving— and he would go off, swinging his right arm around the back of the long front seat, trying to get his hands on one of us, *any* one, and yelling, his voice echoing so loud that my sister Kathleen would cover her ears. My brother Steve and I would cower just beyond the length of his arm, burying our guilty grins in our hands, snickering into the soft upholstery of the back seat until we just could *not* hold it any longer and burst out laughing, setting off a chain reaction, my father swinging his arm around again and bawling us out.

When I was a teenager, a sharpness grew between us. As I sought independence, he became more dedicated to reining me in, or so it seemed to me. We went head to head all the time, bat-

94

tling over things both momentous and trivial—Kent State, Martin Luther King, Janis Joplin, the length of my hair. I remember an argument over what I saw as my *right* to wear Beatle boots.

"I don't care what everybody else is wearing, my kids won't be dressed like hoodlums," vowed my father.

"But I'm the one wearing the clothes, they're my clothes," I protested.

"And I'm the one buying those clothes!" he roared.

Time and again, we would clash—about my falling grades, my clothes, my aimless direction. My siblings would scatter, my mother would post herself inconspicuously in a room nearby, listening, and my father would deliver his latest admonishment, pacing the kitchen floor. It would begin as a stern lecture; then he would pin me against the kitchen counter with his anger, like a blast from a fire hose, and I would listen, wordlessly, taking it, my arms crossed at my chest, my eyes memorizing the pattern in the linoleum floor, despising him for his bluntness and shamed by his reproach. In a fit of frustration, I would strike back, hollering to his face, trying to defend myself. Back and forth, we would yell at each other, until finally one of us would bang out the back door in a fit of frustration.

It was my mother who eventually would thaw the cold war between my father and me, but seldom through direct intervention. My father would stew, I would brood, sometimes for days. But my mother would carry on with her routine conversations, around the dinner table, in front of the TV, making idle observations, relating events of the day: "I was talking to my cousin Mary Ellen, and she's thinking of getting a freezer for the basement. With four kids in the house she just doesn't have room in her refrigerator upstairs anymore." Nothing particularly relevant to my father or me, just *conversation*, the simple act of speaking, of relating, of forming thoughts into words, directing her reports to both of us, deliberately, casting her declarative sentences or posing her questions, exacting an acknowledgment of some kind from us, until we were compelled to join in the conversation, forced to emerge on our knuckles from our damp caves and resume (reasonably) normal behavior. Occasionally, my mother would admonish either my father or me for our stubbornness. Yet rarely was there closure, resolution—a direct discussion of the problem or an admission by one of us that he was wrong. Our stubbornness only perpetuated the arguing.

It would be neither fair nor accurate to say my father had a mean streak. He was kind and charitable, willing to give his time to friends and family without complaint. But sometimes he boiled inside, and when the pressure became too great, he boiled over. "Stress reduction" was not yet a defined term. He could not talk about stress, would not vent it. He kept it in, kept it to himself, lived with it, as many men of his generation were prone to do. He buried himself in his work, his only outlet, his most loyal friend.

While leafing through a stack of old black-and-white photographs at my mother's house a while ago, I came across a snapshot of my father at age twenty. He was scowling at the camera, wearing a look of complete contempt that could stop traffic and scare stray dogs. I don't know what was behind the scowl, but I've seen the expression a thousand times—on the face of my father, and on my own face. It is the face of anger and scorn, all too characteristic of Chandler males. I see it sometimes in my brothers, catch them hollering at their partners or children or each other. Sometimes I see that same scowl on the face of my son—and I feel accountable.

It has become my duty as my son's father—and my father's son—to cut this anger out of the family tree, as if it were a diseased limb or a rotted stump or an unwanted offshoot springing from the ground. The anger, like a malignancy, is hard to carve away. The roots go deep.

The last time I spanked Ben, he was four years old. It was one of only three or four times he was spanked, but it was a bona fide lickin'. I don't know the reason. All I remember is the rage, the ugly outburst directed at this small boy, and the injury I caused. As Ben lay sobbing in his bed, Cathy tugged at his pajamas to check his sore bottom.

"Look what you did to him," she frowned at me. The spanking had left a red welt on his butt in the shape of my hand.

I was sickened by what I'd done, shamed. I never hit him again.

I have made an unspoken pledge to Ben. We will share my father's name, but not his anger. Instead, we will try to emulate the big-hearted humor and generosity that he was also known for.

But that has not always been easy to do. For either of us.

A few weeks before I blew up over the bath towel, it was Ben who was seized by the anger. He lashed out at his mother in a rampage of emotion when she asked, justifiably, when he was going to empty the overflowing trash can in his bedroom.

"Don't tell me what to do!" he shouted, smashing a fist on the top of his dresser and knocking over a framed photograph of himself and his mother. "It's my room and I can take care of myself without you telling me what to do all the time. I'm not a kid anymore."

He turned on his heels, leaving Cathy stunned. But by the afternoon, he had emptied the trash and apologized.

"I'm sorry, Mom," he said. "I've got a big mouth sometimes."

We wrote it off as an adolescent mood swing. But it was more than that. It was anger inherited.

My angry scuffle with Ben throws me into a remorseful funk. Cathy takes Emma to school, and I isolate myself in my basement office for the day, trying to put the episode out of my mind by diving into my work, a self-imposed exile. But by five o'clock, I give up on work for the day. My energy has run out. Wearily, I climb the stairs from my office. In the dining room, the dinner table is set; Emma is sitting at the computer playing a video game.

"Where's Ben?" I ask Cathy.

"Not home from school yet," she says curtly, assembling a salad at the kitchen counter.

I sink into an easy chair in the living room to watch the news. The TV images are trite, predictable, variations of the same old themes—crisis, conflict, controversy, the stuff that TV news is made of, the mug shot of a murder suspect, a deadly car crash, unseasonable weather somewhere far away. The pictures flicker by and barely register as I sit stone-faced in my chair.

A half-hour later, Ben comes through the front door. His jacket over his shoulder and his face slightly flushed, he walks past me without a glance.

"Hello Mom. Hi Emma," he sings out. He tosses his backpack onto his bed and steps into the kitchen. "How was your day, Emma, how was school?"

"Good," she answers. "But my teacher wasn't there today. We had a *stubskitute*."

"A substitute," Ben corrects her.

"Where have you been, hon?" his mother asks.

"I went over to Dan's. We played basketball for a while. Then I went to the library. To do some research."

I decide not to join the conversation. I'm still shaken from the morning's emotional earthquake and can't speak the words I know I need to say.

"Go wash your hands, you two," Cathy says to the children. "We're going to eat in a minute."

We take our places at the dinner table. Ben ignores me. He looks down at his plate or at his mother or sister. He offers little conversation. I remain mute, too, and instead, Cathy and Emma do all the talking.

"I have something to tell you," says Emma in a singsong teasing tone.

"What is it?" asks Cathy.

"Buttons wants to say it," she says, now bashful. Emma pulls her constant companion, her favorite stuffed animal, from her lap and holds it in front of her mouth. In Buttons's make-believe voice, she squeaks: "A boy in my class tried to kiss me."

"What?!"

"Jimmy tried to *kiss* me."

"He tried to kiss you?" Cathy repeats. "In your classroom?"

"And the teacher gave him a time out," says Emma, again using Buttons as her medium. "He's a bad boy."

"So Jimmy was bad today," I affirm.

"He's bad *every* day."

We all laugh, but the laughter is fleeting and strained. The tension is palpable, the same tension that hung in the air around the dinner table after one of my father's explosions, hung as thick as smoke, with no one speaking, no one making eye contact, four kids forcing down our creamed corn and mashed potatoes as fast as we could and then scattering to the wind.

Ben withdraws to his bedroom after the meal. "I've got some homework to do," he says quietly, then closes the door.

Emma takes Buttons up to her bedroom to play, leaving Cathy and me sitting at the table. She looks at me, her elbows on the table, her hands clasped.

"You didn't hit him, did you?"

"No. I didn't hit him. I wouldn't," I say. "But I knocked him down and pushed him around pretty hard." I tug at my lip with my fingers.

"You humiliated him more than you hurt him physically," she says. "His feelings are hurt, you can see it in his face."

"I humiliated myself, too."

"But he didn't deserve that outrage. It devastated him. And Emma—Emma was afraid to look at you this morning."

Cathy shakes her head and glares, visibly annoyed with me. "I just don't get this anger," she says. "I can't stand it."

"And you think I do?" I slouch in my chair, staring into my water glass. "I'm in the wrong, I'm the villain here, I know, and I don't have an excuse. It was a bonehead thing to do. That damned male anger."

She begins stacking the dirty plates on the table. "So what are you going to do? You need to apologize. I can't smooth things over, it's up to you. It's your responsibility."

"Maybe I'll let things cool for a while." I know it's not the answer, but I feel paralyzed.

"If you let them cool for too long, they'll turn cold," Cathy warns. "They'll turn to ice."

The next day is Saturday. The forecast for warm, sunny weather proves to be false. The temperature has dropped into the mid-forties, and slate-gray clouds scud across the sky from the north, a harbinger of winter. I decide that today is the day to install plastic insulation over the living room windows facing the front porch. The clear plastic will help keep the heat in and the cold wind out.

After returning from the hardware store with the supplies, I gather a utility knife, a tape measure, a yardstick, and a stepladder. I pop my head through Ben's open bedroom door. He's sitting on his bed reading.

"Can you give me a hand, Ben? I want to tack some plastic over the front windows."

His eyes flash to me, then back to his book. "Yeah, I guess so." He scoots off the bed, slips on a corduroy shirt, and follows me out to the porch.

The two of us tacked up window plastic last year. We know the drill. It's a half-hour, two-person job.

I clear the toys from the porch, sliding a croquet set to the far end and wheeling Emma's trike into a corner. The porch is screened and covered. Windows open and close to the outside, but there are no storm windows to keep out the bitter winter temperatures.

I unfold the clear plastic and spread it across the wooden floor of the porch. Ben straightens the corners and pulls the plastic tight.

"What's the height of each window?" I ask, and Ben extends the yellow tape measure.

"About seventy-two inches," he says.

"How about width?"

"Thirty."

We measure the distances on the long length of plastic. I run the knife along the edge of the yardstick, dividing the plastic into equal parts. Next, we attach the double-sided tape to the edges of the window. I take two steps up the ladder and Ben hands me a section of plastic. I fasten the top and he fastens the bottom, sealing the plastic tight to the tape, stretching it as we go. It feels good to work with my hands, to move about, to use tools.

All the while, we work in silence. I had hoped that our project would defrost the cold war, loosen the grudge, so that I could more easily talk about it with him. After a blow-out with my father, he invariably would recruit me for some household project—to replace a window screen or trim a hedge along the patio—and slowly, working together, his humor would return and my mood would brighten. I would forget his shouting or he would forget my misdeed. But the words "I'm sorry" never were uttered by either of us. The dysfunction was buried and locked away, rarely sorted out.

I want to get past yesterday, to move on. Last year, Ben and I had fun with this job. It was comical, in fact, a Marx Brothers routine, with me as Groucho, balancing precariously on the ladder and clumsily wrapping myself in tape and plastic, and Ben as Harpo, mocking me behind my back before a giggling Emma inside, watching through the windows. Ben is all business today, working dutifully. The grudge doesn't budge.

Running a hair dryer over the surface of the plastic firms it up and leaves it perfectly transparent. This normally is the moment of satisfaction, the fun part for Ben, who operates the hair dryer. Today he performs the task joylessly, almost robotically, raising his arm and dropping his arm, up and down.

"Are we done here? I've got things to do."

He stalks into the house and back into his room. The afternoon grows colder. We're done for the day. I still can't get out my apology.

The sun returns on Sunday, breaking through the gloom, turning the sky into a mosaic of billowing purple clouds over patches of deep blue and igniting the colors of the falling leaves. It's harvesttime, and Cathy suggests taking a drive into the country to an apple orchard, something we do every year.

"Yes, yes, that's a great idea," I say, and I grab the camera bag from the hall closet.

Ben needs some coaxing, but he agrees to come along. I'm hoping I can make things right with him and lose the anxious feeling that's been gnawing at me all weekend.

Cathy packs the trunk of the car with an armload of jackets and sweaters, and we set out. Our destination is north, a large commercial orchard thirty minutes away. But along the way we see a small sign for another farm—PICK YOUR OWN FRUIT AND VEGETABLES—and we take a detour west down a narrow country road. A mile later, we come to "R Apples" and turn into a gravel driveway.

"Look at all the ducks," Emma calls out as we park the car.

R Apples is a small farm run by Frank Ridley and his family. The Ridleys grow fruit and vegetables and raise free-range poultry. In the fall, they press apples into cider and let customers harvest the crops on their own, charging by the pound.

The wide yard behind the family's brick farmhouse is an adventureland for kids. A hay wagon awaits in the driveway. White-boarded coops hold squawking chickens and turkeys, growing fat for the coming holiday feasts. Geese with fluorescent blue and green stripes on their wings flap about inside a pen. Ducks waddle everywhere, uncaged.

Emma climbs onto a swingset in front of the barn. "Push me, Daddy, push me," she pleads, and I send her happily sailing through the air.

We visit the noisy chickens and feed them dried corn through the wire mesh, and then wind our way through rows and rows of flowers—gladiolas, lilacs, nasturtiums, daisies. Cathy cuts bouquets, a dollar a bunch. Emma and I run along tall columns of sunflowers, as if we've leapt into a painting by Monet, the faces of the flowers smiling down at us.

We take a half-dozen paper bags from the Ridleys and then turn to the sprawling gardens, row after row of vegetables and herbs. Cathy is suddenly a weekend farmer in her bib overalls. She thumps an eggplant and picks an armful of fresh basil for homemade pesto. Ben and Emma kneel in the brown dirt and pop string beans from a row of plants.

"Can I eat one?" Emma asks. I crouch down to her level and kneel. I pick a bean, snap off the ends, and take a bite. The bean is crunchy, sweet, a little gritty from the dirt.

"Now you try," I say, and Emma rips a bean from a stalk and gives it a taste.

"Aaakk." She spits the green pulp into the soil.

"How about you, Ben? Want one?"

"Nah," and he walks over to inspect the sweet corn. He shuns my peace offering.

A minivan pulls into the driveway. Three children spill out, laughing as they race around the chicken coops, calling out at the animals in Spanish. *"Pollos! Mira a los pollos. Y patos!"* Two adults and two teenagers step from the van and walk into the barn. From the farmer, the mother and father are given a stack of paper bags and a wheelbarrow. They walk purposefully toward the rows of vegetables.

The mother, a Mexican American woman about Cathy's age, begins picking green peppers, enormously ripe, and placing them carefully into the bags. A young man in his late teens trails behind with a wheelbarrow, loading bag after bag. Cathy is showing Emma how to pick tomatoes nearby. Cathy smiles at the señora, and she smiles back.

"What are you going to do with all those peppers?" Cathy asks.

She steps from the tomato plants, over a row of beans to the pepper plants. Emma follows. The woman pushes a strand of dark hair from her face. She says several words in Spanish, but Cathy shakes her head.

"Sorry, my Spanish isn't very good."

A teenage girl helps out. "My mother will make chili with these."

"Does she own a restaurant? With so many peppers . . ."

The Mexican mother speaks to her daughter and the girl translates, telling Cathy that she cooks a dish similar to a chili relleno, slicing the peppers in half and filling them with meat and cheese. With all of her family pitching in, she will make dozens of the dish and freeze them for the winter.

"My mother wants to know if you would like the recipe," the girl says to Cathy, and Cathy searches her pockets for a pen and a scrap of paper. A recipe is shared, fellowship sprouts, and I'm suddenly envious of the ease at which women are able to communicate.

I turn to Ben. "Let's go pick some apples," I say.

We leave Cathy and Emma in the pepper rows with their new friends and wander into the orchard, each of us carrying a couple of paper bags. We wade through the grass, tall and brown, the blades sweeping against the legs of our jeans. Each row of apple trees is marked by a small wooden sign nailed to a pole: Cortland, MacIntosh, Jonathan, Harrelson. We start with Harrelsons, pulling the low fruit from a squat, gnarled tree. As we tug at an apple, the tree resists for a moment, its branch bending, then gives up the fruit, the branch flying back into place.

I snag an apple from a branch above my head and take a bite. "Mmm, nice and tart, sour. Good for pies."

We fill one bag and move on to the next row, Jonathans. We both work the same tree. As we pull down the apples, I see that the sky is starting to cloud over again.

"Smells like rain," I say. But Ben doesn't respond.

"You're still mad at me, aren't you."

"I don't know. Maybe I am." He moves on to another tree, looking for better pickings. "I just don't like being pushed around," he says.

"I don't blame you. Not one bit."

I hesitate, but I know this is the time to make amends. "That was wrong of me to push you around like that, Ben. And I am sorry. All I can tell you is I won't lay a hand on you like that again. It frightened me. And it reminded me of my father."

Ben's eyes narrow and he waits for more.

"It's been kind of a tough month for me," I add. "I've been under a little pressure with my work. It's not much of an excuse, but, you know, sometimes when things aren't going so well I take it out on you, and on Cathy and on Emma. All my frustrations— everything gets dumped on the family, because you're the closest to me. It's like when you're in a rotten mood, you'll blow up at your sister or mother or me. Because we're there. It's not right. We both need to work at our tempers. For now, try to let it go. You didn't do anything wrong."

"That's not what you said Friday," he says. "Friday I was just a lazy jerk."

"Well, yes, that you are," I say, trying to ply some humor into the conversation, "but you're also a great kid."

We move along to another row, three bags now filled. Ben's choosy, taking only apples that are perfectly round and flawless. He bites into a MacIntosh, smacks his lips, bites again, and then sends the core flying in my direction. I try to turn away, but I'm not in time. He strikes his target, my stomach.

"*Oooff.*" I double over. Ben grins at his precision and picks up another apple.

"Wait, wait! Truce, truce!" I call out, backing away and grinning myself, and he drops the apple.

A light drizzle is falling. Ben's hair is damp and clinging to his forehead. The raindrops spill down my face. I wipe my eyes with my sleeve. Cathy is calling, standing at the edge of the orchard, a bag of red peppers in her arms: "Come on. It's starting to rain. We've got to go. What are you guys doing?"

We grab the bags of apples and make a beeline to the barn.

Rock 'n' Roll

In the summer before he started high school, Ben and I decided to go to a rock concert together. A local band called the Gufs was generating a considerable buzz. Ben had heard the band on the radio. They fit into the category *alternative rock*, a category that fit with his musical tastes. He had their new CD and wanted to see them live; he'd never been to a rock concert before. But he couldn't get any of his friends to go with him. None of them liked the band.

"I'll go with you," I offered one day.

"You'd go?" he asked with a puzzled look that said, *But you're my dad.* "You *want* to go?"

"Sure. It'll be fun. I've heard you play that Gufs album a few times. They're a pretty good band. I'd like to see them. I think we should go."

I don't know if this pleased him or annoyed him. Going to a rock concert with your father could be a serious liability for a teenager. Each generation's musical tastes are supposed to disagree with its parents'. Sinatra to Elvis, the Beatles to the Sex Pistols, each new wave is a sign of rebellion, of drawing the line between young and old, of breaking away. How could Ben break away if *his* musical tastes became *my* musical tastes?

But the stage had been set for a while now. Our tastes had blended for years. Ben knew—and even *liked*—the music of the Beatles. He grew up listening to Hendrix and the Who, Jefferson

Airplane and the Dead, Joni Mitchell and James Taylor, Clapton, Springsteen, Stevie Wonder, folk, rock, even country—music that Cathy and I had known since our teenage years, music that had been the soundtracks of our lives, together and apart. My obsession with collecting the complete works of Bob Dylan had become easy fodder for endless razzing by Ben and his mother. Yet he appreciated the power of Dylan's songs. Back in seventh grade, he incorporated the lyrics of Dylan's "Masters of War" into a history project.

I, meanwhile, had followed Ben's progression from the songs of Disney and Raffi to Nirvana, REM, Wilco, and Counting Crows. Although I wouldn't play his music by choice, I've tried to keep my ears and mind open to whatever is playing on Ben's stereo.

Sometimes that's not easy.

I've seen Ben bring home CDs bearing "parental advisory" labels that warn of objectionable lyrics. I've read the lyric sheets (squinting at the fine print without my reading glasses) and I'm aware of the objectionable words, words that he's heard before but rarely repeats. I believe Ben can handle the objectionable words. So far, they haven't driven him into spells of blasphemy or fits of cursing. I've also read lyrics that are sexually explicit and others that seem to incite violence. The lyrics of the Dead Kennedys, for instance, can be stark and provocative. But the lyrics are satirical. When John Lennon sang "Happiness is a warm gun," I got the point. Ben can handle satire. Ben can handle provocative.

"Going to a concert with your dad would be like going to a concert with your history teacher or something," Ben said to me, not the worst of comparisons. Yet he agreed to go.

The Gufs concert was an outdoor show at Milwaukee's Summerfest, an eleven-day music festival on the shores of Lake Michigan. We'd drive down to the lakefront, buy tickets at the gate, grab dinner at a concession stand, and find a couple of seats somewhere in the grandstand.

"Don't wait up, Mom," Ben says, and out the door we go.

We arrive at the festival grounds just after six o'clock. A line of people snakes along the edge of a chain-link fence and leads to the turnstiles into the Rock Stage, one of a dozen different venues at the festival. The line is thick, a cable of people in their teens and twenties, all dressed in urban black—T-shirts, tank tops, jeans, boots—with hair cut close to the scalp or in dreadlocks or dyed orange, with pierced lips, pierced eyebrows, pierced navels, pierced parts unseen.

There aren't many things I will wait in line for anymore. A half-hour wait to be seated in an exceptionally good restaurant is about my limit. Waiting in line to buy overpriced concert tickets became unacceptable years ago; I'd rather buy the CD. But this evening, as I stand here dressed in my baggy khaki shorts, white running shoes, and Greenpeace T-shirt, I see that I'm not the only geezer in line with these kids. Scattered about are other parents with their own teenage sons and daughters. I make eye contact with another dad, a man also in running shoes and shorts, and we smile. We connect, two middle-agers, bearing the bother with cool indifference, as much as any perfectly patient parent can who's waiting to pass through the turnstiles with twenty-five thousand grunged-out Gen Xers on too much Mountain Dew. Ben behaves as any perfectly bored teenager can with Dad on Board, his back to me, blue jeans too long and shabby, silently sulking, searching the crowd on the off-chance that he will see someone, *anyone*, from his school to talk to.

There's no adequate word in the English language to describe the separation that cleaves teenagers from parents. The term "generation gap" was popular decades ago, but it's no longer apt. As I see it, today, from the vantage point of a parent, it's more than a gap. It's a fissure that opens during an earthquake, a fissure that swallows your child whole and then quickly closes, leaving you wondering what happened to your baby.

Some say the quake is inevitable and advise parents to let their children go, let them drop into the abyss alone. But I'm not sure I want to give up my son to adolescence without some resistance. If nothing else, I will know him better than my parents knew me, know his interests, know the books he reads, the movies he sees, the classes he takes, the friends he keeps. I want to know his taste in clothes, in art, in food, in cars, in magazines, in music. I want to watch his politics take shape. I want to know how he thinks.

"What did you learn at school today?" is my pat question every evening at the dinner table. For as many times as Ben will answer "Nothin'," he will give me a full and fascinating rundown of a physics experiment he did on the Second Law of Thermodynamics (*entropy is increasing in the universe*), or he'll launch into a discussion he had in his government class on the Bill of Rights, or he'll summarize a report he's writing on Edgar Allan Poe. All I have to do is ask.

The turnstiles finally turn, and Ben and I are thrust into a sea of people. Ben is one of the younger fans in the crowd, I'm one of the older. I put my hand on his shoulder so we're not separated and steer him toward the side bleachers, moving him against the tide. We're jammed tight, claustrophobic, pushed forward half-step by half-step. Finally we reach the risers and find a couple of seats.

"All right. We made it," Ben says.

"And just in time," I say, looking around. The grandstands are nearly full. The show is sold out.

We have a clear view of the stage. Behind us in the distance, we can see the lights of the midway, a double Ferris wheel swinging around and around, and from a nearby stage I hear the loping beat of a reggae band. To our right, we look out to Lake Michigan, steel blue water in the evening light, and to our left, at the gleaming city skyline.

Milwaukee once was the epitome of small time, characterized by polka bands, Friday-night fish fries, a tavern on every corner, and odd twosomes that were hard to live down—beer and brats, Laverne and Shirley, Harley and Davidson. Recently, though, Milwaukee has been coming into its own. It's a big-little town, with a revitalized downtown and an unspoiled waterfront, a city of festivals and parks. It's a city that's cautious yet open to change, hard-headed but open-hearted. We take our time, we wait our turn, and we try to get along, wary of the push-and-shove, every-man-for-himself attitude of bigger cities.

After a delay—there's always a delay—the Gufs take the stage, two guitarists, a bass player, and a drummer, four men in their twenties dressed in what might be bowling shirts and black jeans. They plug in and tune up, intermittently sending feedback screaming across Lake Michigan. *Shreeeeeeeppp!* A speaker the size of the Parthenon faces us fifty feet away. We cover our ears.

The band opens with its hit single, a song called "Smile." A knot of young women swarm the aisles, singing, dancing, the pulse of the music drawing them closer to the stage, the deep beat of the bass loud enough to start—or stop—a heart. Ben nods his head and slaps his leg to the rhythm, mouthing the words to the songs he knows, but never singing out loud and never daring to dance. I feel out of place, rocking to the music of a band young enough to be my children. But I strum on an air guitar, mimicking the lead guitarist, wrinkling my face and thrusting out my bottom lip. Ben snickers at my dumb antics, waving me away. It's too loud to speak, too crowded to breathe. Just the way it ought to be.

One of the first rock shows I saw was a concert by Jimi Hendrix. I went with my girlfriend Jill. We were seniors in high school, wearing love beads and leather sandals. I have few recollections of the concert. Some friends delivered us to the front doors of the auditorium, I remember that much. I also know that drugs were a significant part of the show. (*"Have you ever been experienced?"* Hendrix dared us.) Jill and I shared some hallucinogens that night, orange mescaline, I believe, so named because the tablet itself was orange and also because the drug was supposed to cast an orange psychedelic glow on everything in sight, according to the friend who turned us on. Jill and I split a hit before we entered the auditorium, and by the time the warm-up act started to play, we were tripping all over each other, the pupils of our eyes the size of bass drums, the grins on our faces awestruck and foolish.

I don't recall seeing an orange glow, but I do have an image fixed in my mind of Hendrix onstage, bigger than life. Jill and I had abandoned our seats and had flocked to a side aisle with a couple dozen other stoned-out freaks, a shout away from the band. Jimi's guitar pierced us like a million darts. He grimaced as he played, fingering the guitar behind his back, picking the strings with his teeth, the bending notes shrieking like sirens.

Jill danced in circles, her hands extended over her head, her fingertips leaving trails in the air. Strobes flickered in the smoky darkness, and when we looked into each other's faces, ghostly and wild in the white-heat flash, we laughed uncontrollably until the wind was sucked out of our lungs. I lost the notes for a second, for a minute, for a year, drifting backwards in slow-motion from the stage, away and away and away . . . and back again finally, feet stomping and all senses overloading. The smell of marijuana mixed with patchouli. Feedback swirled around the ceiling of the concert hall. Colored spotlights ignited Jimi's rainbow Nehru jacket, a headband tight around his Afro. And for the finale, as one last mind-blowing feat, he doused his Stratocaster with lighter fluid and struck a match, sending us to delirium.

The Gufs take a break, and Ben and I stand to stretch. Ben digs a water bottle out of his backpack. The sun is down. The crowd has settled into a mellow stupor.

"What's that smell?" Ben asks.

I turn around. Behind us, high in the bleachers, a young man with a ponytail is tokin' on a joint, a number, a doobie, a reefer.

"Umm, that's a marijuana cigarette," I say to Ben. "That guy behind us is smoking pot."

Ben spins his head.

"Smell familiar, Dad?" He entraps me with his question.

"Well, yes, it's familiar, sure. But that was a long time ago. A *long* time ago." I turn the question on him. "Does it smell familiar to you?"

"No." He answers indignantly, as if accused.

"Ever smell it before?"

"Nope. I haven't. You're the one who recognized it."

"You're right, I was that kid with the ponytail once. But those were different times, it was a different world. There seemed to be more of an innocence back then. Those were the days of peace signs and love-ins, not bomb-sniffing German shepherds patrolling high school hallways and drive-by shootouts on city streets."

"So drugs weren't a problem when you were my age?"

"I'm not saying that. Drugs were dangerous, dangerous then, dangerous now. And illegal. They can mess people up. Look at Jimi Hendrix. Or Kurt Cobain. The list goes on and on. But so much was happening then. People were experimenting. Society was changing—gender roles were stood upside down, systems were challenged. Art, politics, education, business, everywhere you looked, people were trying new things. You know that. I don't have to sound like your history teacher." And I let it drop, looking back toward the concert stage.

It's difficult to talk to Ben about my drug use. I will own up to using drugs, and without apology. It was part of my past. I can't take it back. And I won't. Drugs were plentiful and they were fun when I was a teenager. Yet I will also admit to some very stupid moves. Getting high at school, getting high behind the wheel of a car—I can't justify it, can't defend it.

In some ways, kids using drugs today are doing penance for the sins of the baby boom generation. Parents of the sixties have a problem saying no to something they were doing themselves. When we do say no, when we preach against the same illegal drugs that we once used, we look hypocritical. So we duck the issue and abide with the contradiction. Cathy and I have sat Ben down for frank discussions about drugs. He's been run through

113

the DARE propaganda. He's seen the public service announce-
ments: "This is your brain on drugs . . ." Ben knows the risks,
we're confident of that. But lectures will go only so far to keep
him straight. We have never suspected him of using drugs. I can
only hope we know him well enough to recognize the warning
signs if he is.

Ben is high on the energy of the band. The audience now is on its
feet, and Ben is standing on his seat. Colored spotlights flood the
stage. The smell of dope is thick. But my attention begins to drift.
Between songs, I can hear from behind the grandstand the strains
of a Chicago blues band on a nearby stage, a band I know from
younger days. And for a minute, I'm tempted to slip away, to find
my old music.

The crowd calls the Gufs back for a second encore. It's been a
long show, my ears are ringing, my back is sore from the backless
metal bleacher bench, and I could use a beer. But Ben is wide-
eyed, stamping his feet now and clapping his hands—almost
dancing—and I'm infected by his excitement, tuning in to his
tunes. I've enjoyed the concert, even singing along on the chorus
of a song or two that I recognized.

With a long, deafening finish to their last song, the band finally bids the crowd good night, and we head for the gates. We shuffle through the turnstiles, the mob scattering around us, people
howling in the moonlight.

"It was good, it was a good show," I say. "I think the band was
even better live than on the record."

"You mean CD, Dad. They don't make records anymore," Ben
reminds me.

"Yeah. Well, I'm glad we came."

"Me, too. It was great. Kind of loud, but it was cool." He
pauses with a thought. "Maybe we can come back again. There's
another band playing this weekend that I'd like to see."

"I don't know," I hesitate. "I'll tell you what: Next time, it's my choice. The next concert we go to has to be someone from my era, someone from my record collection."

He looks at me warily but nods. "Okay, maybe. But no country music."

Months later, a week before the Christmas break, I'm lugging musical equipment up the back steps of an Italian restaurant, a suburban roadie for my own two-man band. I'm carrying a couple of mike stands and a beat-up guitar case, and my partner in song, Kris, has got a grip around a speaker cabinet.

"Who's idea was this anyway?" I say. "You didn't say anything about heavy lifting. This is work."

As a test of our creative mettle—and as a nod to our Baby Boomer anthem *So you wanna be a rock 'n' roll star*—Kris and I have formed a folk-rock duet. We call ourselves the Dharma Boys, lifted from Jack Kerouac's novel *The Dharma Bums*. We've booked ourselves into a few local bars and coffeehouses, and tonight, a Friday night, we're playing a gig at Vinny's Restaurant in the town of Delafield, west of the city.

The restaurant is designed to resemble a Colonial farmhouse, with hardwood floors and red-and-white tablecloths. Adjacent to an upstairs dining room is a small bar and lounge, furnished with a sofa, comfortable armchairs, floor lamps, and Oriental rugs. Vinny Tomasello, the proprietor, books musical acts a couple of times a week. An old Deadhead, Vinny rides a Harley, wears his hair long, and still loves the old tunes.

I open my guitar case and lean the instrument on its stand. I play acoustic guitar, a Martin guitar I've had now for more than twenty-five years. Kris plays guitar and mandolin. He blows harmonica too, blues harp on three or four songs. We've been singing together since we were in college; our voices blend like brothers'.

115

This is our first night at Vinny's. The atmosphere is informal and intimate, the crowd is small, and Cathy and the kids are sitting front and center, cheering on the old man. But I've got stage fright. My throat is dry and my palms are clammy.

I think of my musical background. I started taking guitar lessons when I was about thirteen from Mr. Forester, who ran a music studio with his wife in the basement of their suburban ranch home. The basement was musty, redolent of mildew and old newspaper, and Mr. Forester's breath was worse. The lessons were painfully dull. After six months, Mr. Forester's students were required to perform in a recital in the auditorium of a local church. I knew two songs, "I Love You Truly" and "Go Tell Aunt Rhody." I played them terribly, my stubby fingers numbed by nervousness. Soon after the recital, I pleaded with my parents to let me quit.

When I was a junior in high school, I took up the guitar again. This time, the lessons were less formal. My friend Paul taught me to play. Paul came from a family of musicians. His mother taught piano, his mother and father sang in the church choir, and an older brother played bassoon. Paul had gotten a second-hand guitar somewhere and painted it red, white, and blue, stars and stripes forever. I bought a used guitar for twenty-five dollars and painted the body all white. We learned how to strum the chords of Dylan, Donovan, and Peter, Paul, and Mary, and worked out the harmonies of Simon and Garfunkel, the Byrds, and Crosby, Stills and Nash. Over one weekend, we figured out the guitar parts to the entire side-two opus of the Beatles' *Abbey Road*. For a social studies project in our senior year, Paul and I learned a handful of old cowboy songs and labor union tunes—songs such as Woody Guthrie's "Union Maid" and "Deportees." Our high school teachers arranged for us to perform before the school body. We aced the course.

Kris and I began playing together three years later. We were roommates at the University of Wisconsin in Milwaukee. In the living room of our flat, I passed along to Kris most of what I'd learned from Paul, spending time that should have been spent studying. When I eventually moved west, my playing lapsed. But since moving back home to Milwaukee, I've played regularly with both of them.

I open a file folder of lyric sheets, printed in large print, and arrange them on a music stand. I can't rely on my middle-aged memory anymore. I fix my microphone to a stand and plug the cord into the sound board. Kris sets the tone levels for the instruments and places a glass fishbowl on a small table in front of us for tips. He wears white pants and a colorful Hawaiian shirt, going for that Jimmy Buffett escapism as winter takes hold. I'm dressed down in blue jeans, a black turtleneck, and a pair of black work boots, looking like some brooding beatnik folk singer, in Cathy's opinion. We're wedged together in a corner of the lounge, no stage, no colored spotlights or sophisticated equipment, just a small sound system to boost our voices and instruments. Amid the sound of clinking glasses and rattling silverware, we tune our guitars and check the volume.

I take a sip of beer and speak into my microphone.

"Testing testing one two. Okay, we're gonna start." A short blast of feedback suddenly bites into the room, and I back away from my mike. Kris adjusts the volume and we try again.

"Good evening, welcome to Vinny's," Kris smiles to the audience, a bit more polished and professional than I am. "We're the Dharma Boys. We're going to play some acoustic music for the next couple of hours. We'd like to kick things off with a tune by Bob Dylan."

The bartender, a college student, gives us a thumbs up. Cathy, Emma, and Ben clap their hands, Ben only halfheartedly, trying to maintain an air of cool boredom. Kris's wife, Diane, flashes a supportive grin, and we break into the opening chords of "You Ain't Going Nowhere." Playing is automatic. The song has been part of our repertoire for years, for decades. Kris sings the verses as I take the harmony on the chorus.

Ooooweee, ride me high . . .

Kris trades a harmonica solo with my guitar solo, and we end with a flourish, a strong strum of our guitars. The crowd applauds generously.

Kris leads the show. "Kurt is going to sing one now."

I take another sip of beer to fortify my nerves. Even performing with a partner, I feel defenseless in front of the crowd. As I sing the next tune, I search the faces of the audience for their reaction. When I get to the second verse, I stumble some, forgetting the words and repeating the first, but no one seems to notice, and again, the applause is generous, a little louder now. Emma is on her feet, shaking a maraca and dancing on the rug. Ben watches from a chair, slouching under his flannel shirt. He has heard me play at home but never in public. The spectacle of father-as-performer, as wanna-be rocker, must crack him up, maybe even embarrass him some.

"Yeeahhh, all right, all *right*," Ben says, hamming it up between songs, trying to fluster me.

"We'd like to do a country song now," I announce and break into a few chords from a Garth Brooks tune. But I stop short, smiling at Ben. He's not amused.

"Booo," he cups his hands around his mouth. Cathy shuts him up with an elbow to his side.

The banter relaxes me a bit. Emma asks for her favorite, a Beatles tune she's heard us perform before. "Do the falling song," she yells out, and we honor her request, playing "I've Just Seen a Face."

Falling, yes I am falling . . .

The harmonies grow stronger throughout the night and we move through our set list with ease, swapping vocals, singing songs by John Prine, Tom Petty, Neil Young, the Beatles, cover songs the audience recognizes mixed with songs of our own. Kris has written a couple of original compositions, and just a few weeks ago I wrote my first song, drawing on lyrics that had been sitting in a drawer for years, lyrics that began as a birthday poem to Cathy, titled "All Over You." Kris plays mandolin and adds a harmony.

You're in the back of my mind
I'm in the palm of your hand
You're running up and down my spine . . .

The song is very well received, my three biggest fans clapping the loudest. The stage fright that gripped me earlier has vanished. The tightness in my voice is gone and the notes come freely. The bronze strings of my guitar are gleaming and silky under my fingers, my fingertips fitting perfectly to the fretboard. I shuffle my feet as we play, dancing in my big boots to the chunking rhythms of our guitars. I feel a little self-conscious to be having this much fun. But time and age disappear. I'm having a blast.

As we sing, I look around the room and I see that many in the audience are singing along—bald-headed guys in powder-blue monogrammed golf sweaters and women in pricey tunics and sensible shoes mouthing the words to "Margaritaville," whistling along to "Me and Julio Down by the Schoolyard," singing out loud the happy and rollicking chorus of "Brown Eyed Girl."

Do you remember whennnnn . . . we used to sing . . .

Our soft-rock repertoire has struck a memory chord for this crowd. These baby boomers, our contemporaries, still want to rock 'n' roll. Kris and I are living out a fantasy as the Dharma Boys—and, by proxy, the fantasies of half the folks in this room, the fantasies of a generation. Hope I die before I get old? Nah, not me. I'm gonna rock around the clock, gonna be playing when I'm sixty-four and beyond, right into the nursing home.

The exuberance, the passion, the *youth* doesn't have to fade away with age. A middle-aging criminal defense lawyer I know writes fan letters to Eric Clapton in the courtroom during lulls in trials. Another friend who's worked as a newspaper editor for more than twenty-five years bought himself a digital piano so he could relearn the Beatles tunes he used to play. Music, he says, is his psychic reset switch. And my brother Steve and his eleven-year-old son, Nick, have begun taking electric guitar lessons together.

It's only rock 'n' roll, but we like it.

The Dharma Boys finish the night with three songs for three generations: For the Generation Xers in the house, we play "Rain King" by Counting Crows. For the old hippies among us, we play the Grateful Dead's theme song "Truckin'." And for the hipsters from the fifties, we play the Everly Brothers' "Bye Bye Love," our two-part harmonies strong and soaring.

The crowd claps and cheers. There are smiles all around the room. Vinny pumps our hands, promising to book us again. Cathy, Diane, and the kids gather around to congratulate us. Ben gives us a high five, finally won over by our act.

"Sounded really good, you guys," he says. Felt really good, too, the music soul-satisfying, the response flattering, the energy in the room more of a rush than most highs I can remember. Music will help keep me centered.

My appearance, though, does not fit the persona of a rock star, as Ben points out on the ride home. He offers some advice for the next gig.

"You need to grow your hair longer, Dad," he says, eyeing me head to toe with a serious expression. "And next time wear a fancy shirt."

I'll ignore his advice on the hair. Been there, done that, not much left to work with anyway. But he's probably right about the shirt.

A Florida Vacation

Midway through Ben's freshman year, Cathy and the kids and I bid adieu to the icy Wisconsin winter. We can't afford airfare for four, so we rent a silver Thunderbird, load it with luggage, junk food, Crayolas, a ream of drawing paper, and a few books-on-tape, and point the long car south to Florida, home of Cathy's mother.

Two days later, we're poolside.

"Come on in, Daddy, come *in*."

I can think of no better tonic than warm sunshine on bare skin, and a crystal-clear pool of water.

"What are you waiting for, Dad?" Ben says. "Just do it. It's not even cold."

I hang my toes over the tile lip at the deep end of the pool, cock both arms back, take a deep breath, and jump.

As I expected, Ben was suckering me about the water temperature. I spring from the bottom of the pool and break the surface with a gasp, my lungs robbed of air by the shock. But as intended, my splash was big enough to send a shower of water raining down on Cathy's pink shoulders as she lay nearby on a plastic beach chair, a thick book in her hand.

"Naahhhh! You jerk," she shouts at me, affectionately. Our vacation is heartily underway.

The pool is in a townhouse development where Cathy's mother lives. Red bougainvillea blossom on arching trellises along a

121

peach-colored stucco wall. Beach chairs and tables are arranged around a small courtyard. Except for a few tiny green lizards that run in and out of the flower beds, the courtyard and pool are ours. Our exuberance and pale skin mark us as tourists.

Emma laughs and begins to dog paddle toward me, two front teeth now missing from her smile, her chin up, dark bangs standing on end, hands churning. She's fearless in the water. Though she doesn't yet know how to swim, she's persistent, which counts for half the battle.

"Kick your feet," Ben coaches, "keep kicking."

He sits on the top step of the pool, the late morning sun drying the water from his back. He's slim, now growing more proportionally than he was a year ago, when his feet seemed elephantine on the ends of his stunted limbs. His body is mostly devoid of hair, unmarked, unblemished. By contrast, my chest and shoulders are covered with a furry mane, now turning white. A scar on my shoulder is a reminder of a small carcinoma that was removed a couple of years ago. My only growth is my mid-forties paunch.

"Is this paradise or what?" I say to Cathy, and she sighs ecstatically, her nose back in her book.

I wade toward Emma, catching her under her arms just as she begins to sink. She scoots away from me and hops to the side of the pool, water up to her lower lip. She hangs on to the side with one hand and begins paddling around the perimeter.

"You're a daredevil," I say, following alongside as she splashes on.

"Emma, let me teach you how to float on your back," Ben says. He pushes off the step and swims to her side.

"I'll get water in my nose."

"No, I'll hold you up. Let's try." He places an arm under her legs and a hand under her back, laying her on the surface.

"Put your arms out at your sides," says the big brother. "Now just relax, and tilt your head back."

"What?" Her ears are underwater.

"Just relax." He releases his hold. "See. You're floating. You're floating."

"What?"

I swim three or four laps and take a chair next to Cathy's. On a round table are my sunglasses and a Travis McGee mystery by John D. McDonald, perfect Florida reading.

"You're burning up," I tell Cathy, trying to cover her legs with a towel. But she throws it off.

"I'll risk it," she says. "I just want to lie here and simmer for an hour."

We travel to south Florida once a year to visit Cathy's family. Her mother, Shirlee Brun, lives ten minutes from the Atlantic in Boca Raton with her husband, Joe Brun. Joe and Shirlee were married a year before Cathy and I; Joe was a widower and Shirlee a widow. Cathy's father died in 1968, when she was four-teen. Her only sibling, an older sister, lives in Boston, but her aunt and cousin also live in Boca Raton, so each of our annual visits takes on the semblance of a family reunion, marked by a tournament of dinner parties and never-ending group photos. I play a multiple role at these gatherings: the photographer, bar-tender, and chief joke listener, nodding and groaning at every bad line that's delivered my way. "Guy walks into a bar with a chicken and orders a drink . . ."

Shirlee is a strong-willed woman who has made a living on her own since the death of Cathy's father. She worked as an art instructor in New Jersey, her home state, before moving to Florida in the early 1970s, and for years she ran an art gallery in Miami. In her gallery one day, she met Joe. Joe was born in France and resettled in the United States decades ago. He worked as a Hollywood cinematographer from the 1940s to the 1960s and was nominated once for an Academy Award. His scrapbook bulges with photographs of himself on various movie sets with celebrities, including actors John Wayne and Kim Novak and directors Robert Wise and Howard Hawks. After his retirement from moviemaking, Joe became a painter. From Shirlee's gallery, he sold his cubist-style oil paintings of French landscapes, parades, and portraits. Ten years ago, Shirlee sold the gallery and started a small catering business out of her home. At seventy-five, she continues to cook nearly every day, and at eighty-nine, Joe continues to paint.

"Yoohoo? Who's hungry?" Shirlee stands at the courtyard gate and beckons. "I'm putting lunch on the table soon," she says. "Dry off and come in."

"No! Not yet!" Emma protests, and she plunges her head underwater. But Ben is already wrapping himself in a towel.

"Maybe we'll come back to the pool this afternoon, honey," says Cathy, and we gather our belongings. We walk across the street and return to the townhouse.

Before sitting for lunch, I go to the refrigerator for something to drink. "Maybe a cold beer," I say. "It's barely noon, but what the hell, I'm on vacation."

I swing open the refrigerator door and a grapefruit drops to the floor. Top to bottom, the refrigerator is packed with food. Three cartons of juice, two cartons of milk, three half-empty bottles of white wine, bagels and English muffins, cream cheese and sour cream, pasta sauce by the half gallon, more than a dozen bottles of salad dressing and five different mustards, olives, pickles, jalapeño peppers, stir-fry seasoning, jams and jellies and pastes and relishes, garlic cloves by the fistful, baskets of fresh mushrooms and giant red peppers, citrus fruit of every color, and leftovers in covered containers of all shapes and sizes—all stacked precariously atop of each other on the shelves. Maybe I'm not that thirsty after all, I tell myself, looking into this precarious labyrinth of food, unable to see a beer.

But I crouch down and enter the maze, cautiously removing one item at a time, like playing the child's game Mousetrap, where one wrong move can tumble the entire puzzle. I place a dish of glazed carrots and a plastic tub of homemade curried chicken salad on the floor, balance half a cantaloupe on my knee, and grasp the neck of a brown bottle of beer between my forefinger and thumb. I restack the food, gently close the refrigerator door, and open my prize.

We lay towels on the chairs to protect them from our damp bathing suits and sit at the table in the dining room. The spread looks like three lunches.

"Kurt, try some pear salad," Shirlee says, handing me a salad bowl filled with Romaine lettuce and succulent sliced pears.

Suddenly I'm famished. Emma is eating a hot dog. Ben is going for the curried chicken on pita bread, a Shirlee original. Cathy is sampling the pear salad with leftover pasta. Joe is eating a tuna salad made with olives, cayenne, and other spices.

"How did you like your swim, little girl?" Joe asks, smiling adoringly at Emma, a French accent notable in his soft voice. He sits at the head of the table, casually dressed in a polo shirt and a pair of jeans, a short man, thin light hair combed back. The index finger on his left hand is missing, the result of some unexplained accident decades ago.

"Good," she says between bites, her hair still wet from the pool. "I was floating. On my back."

"She's a beauty, isn't she?" he says to Shirlee. "And what about you, big boy?" He turns to Ben. "How was the water? Was it warm enough?"

"Warm enough for me. Not for Mom."

"Cathy, try the chicken salad," says Shirlee. "And Kurt?" She passes the salad bowl to me again. The force feed has begun.

"Ben," Shirlee says, "how would you like to help me for an hour or so this afternoon? I've got a huge order of crab cakes that has to be delivered to a restaurant in Miami tomorrow."

"How many?" Cathy asks.

"Fifty."

"Sure, I'll help," says Ben. "I'd like that."

Ben has become an able cook himself, learning by observing his mother and grandmother. I remember him, even at age nine or ten, standing on a footstool at the stove in our kitchen, scrambling eggs or browning French toast for breakfast. "You'll make someone a good husband someday," his mother beams whenever he cooks, making him blush.

After lunch, Ben reports to the kitchen for his mess-hall duty. Shirlee is leaning on the counter, a wooden spoon in her hand, her apron daubed with specks of yellow curry sauce, the sign of a working chef. In a metal bowl half the size of a bathtub, she begins to mix crab meat, bread crumbs, red peppers, green peppers, onions, and a garden of spices. As Ben watches, she scoops a palmful of the mixture from the bowl, weighs it on a kitchen scale, rolls it into a ball, and presses it flat with her two hands.

"Just like that," she says. "It should only be about an inch and a half thick. No bigger."

Ben tries, flattening a cake with his palm, pushing his left hand into his right.

"I think I've got the technique. It's kind of fun, actually."

"You think so, try making a couple hundred in one day."

The two of them become an assembly line, Shirlee rolling the mix into round balls, Ben flattening the balls into cakes, Shirlee loading the baking pans into a commercial-sized oven, and Ben removing the finished product from the baking pans with a spatula. In short order, the room smells like the state of Maryland, with crab cakes covering every level surface in the kitchen.

"Ben, you are really starting to grow up," Shirlee says, looking at the teenager as she rolls the last of the mix into a ball. "Since I saw you last summer, you've shot up three inches. And meanwhile I've shrunk." She stretches her neck, trying to somehow recover a lost inch or two.

"I'm still catching up to my friends, though. Almost all of them are taller than me."

"I remember when you were a baby as if it were yesterday. You were a perfect little boy, the best. I flew out to Colorado to visit a few weeks after you were born. I had to see my grandson, my only grandson. For some reason, God knows why, your parents decided to have a picnic. In the mountains, yet. It was a sunny day but there was still snow on the ground. So there I am, stumbling along this snowy trail in the mountains with my pocketbook over my arm, and your father is carrying you in this little straw basket, a baby basket that someone bought for you, swinging you along with one hand like you're a sack of potatoes. And as we're walking, he suddenly loses his grip and you go tumbling to the ground. I almost died. Luckily, you landed on a little mound of pine needles and it cushioned your fall. But I could have killed your father."

"I guess I don't remember that," Ben says and laughs.

Cathy's family is Jewish. But at Cathy's request, Shirlee and Joe join in the exchange of presents on Christmas morning whenever we visit, for the benefit of their grandchildren. This year, as a drop site for jolly old Santa Claus, Shirlee has decorated a small, living pine tree, no more than two feet tall, with tiny lights and ornaments. She has mounted the baby pine tree on a footstool in her dining room, and beside the tree she's placed two huge, red poinsettia plants. Already, gift-wrapped boxes have begun to appear.

At home, our family celebrates both Christmas and Hanukkah, but in a loose fashion. According to the matriarchal custom of Judaism, the children of a Jewish woman are raised as Jews. Cathy does not belong to a temple. Her practice of Judaism waned when she hit adolescence, due partly to the death of her father. Today, she disagrees with many of the laws of orthodox or conservative Jews and eschews their rituals, yet she identifies strongly with Jewish culture and history.

"Your faith comes from within," she has told Ben, "and whether you worship with a yarmulke on your head or choose to eat a certain kind of meat is not what's important. To be loving and kind, to help others, these are the things that are important."

Ben's religious instruction has been inconsistent. While living in Minneapolis, he attended Sunday school for three or four years at a reformed temple. He learned some rudimentary Hebrew, and we celebrated with a Seder at Passover each year at the home of Jewish friends, me struggling with the Hebrew words as we read aloud the story of the Pharaoh and the slaves to our children.

My Catholicism likewise lapsed in my teenage years and then disappeared altogether. I'd had enough of being told what I could not do. What I saw as hypocrisy within the church turned me away from religion as a whole. I questioned the existence of a deity. If there is a God, I reasoned, He need not waste His almighty breath on me.

I have friends who have studied Tibetan Buddhism and other eastern religions. I have friends who pray to angels, who pray to the forest, who have followed the movement of the planets and the stars, who have sought the teachings of spiritual gurus. Like many Baby Boomers, I'm intrigued by some of the New Age practices and beliefs. I also think that living according to some of the Christian tenets generally can be a good thing. But I continue to be an unbeliever. Except for weddings and funerals, I rarely go inside a church. I remain on the periphery of religion.

For our children's edification, Cathy and I have taken them to services and ceremonies in both churches and synagogues. My mother has taken Emma to Mass at her Catholic church and explains to her the significance of particular holy days and sacraments. We observe the commercial holiday traditions, both Christian and Jewish, as they come around on the calendar. Christmas and Hanukkah, Easter and Passover—they are not disregarded, yet neither are they greatly rejoiced.

Before leaving home, Ben and Emma lit the candles of the menorah for the eight days of Hanukkah. Each night, Cathy placed the brass candelabrum on the table and handed a book of matches to Ben. I watched from the wings as Ben struck a match and guided Emma's small hand over the menorah as she put flame to wick.

"What are the candles for?" Emma asked.

"They're to celebrate Hanukkah," Ben explained. "Hanukkah is known as the Festival of Lights. This candle holder is called a menorah. It's a symbol of people who are Jewish. Like you."

"Why are there eight candles?" she asked.

"It's a tradition. There are eight days of Hanukkah. The candles stand for the eight days that some holy oil burned in a temple a long, long time ago."

Shirlee and Joe have been an influence on Ben and Emma's understanding of Judaism. Shirlee relates stories of Jewish traditions to the children and translates Yiddish expressions. Joe can be quite cynical toward organized religion, a trait that is manifest amusingly in his art. He especially likes to poke fun at the venerated images of rabbis and nuns, depicting them as comical figures in several of his paintings. But if Joe has no use for organized religion, he is passionate about his Jewish lineage. He left his homeland of France before the Second World War, but speaks somberly of aunts and uncles who died at the hands of the Nazis.

Ben seldom brings up the subject of God. Like many teenagers, he's sorting out his own beliefs. Copies of *The Joys of Yiddish* and *The Jewish World* can be found on his bookshelf, along with Marx's *Das Kapital*. Judaism has become some part of Ben's selfhood, something he's glad to recognize and proud to share, even if he doesn't entirely have it worked out yet.

Ben and Emma stand before the miniature pine tree in Grandma Shirlee's dining room.

"Will Santa know where to put the presents?" Emma asks.

"Of course," Shirlee plays along, and she takes Emma into her lap. "On Christmas Eve," she tells her, "we're going to take you to see a house in the neighborhood that's all lit up. Colored Christmas lights all over the yard, hundreds of lights, thousands.

And there's music playing, and puppets to see, and dolls that move. We'll walk around and look at all the lights, okay?"

This seems to allay Emma's concerns about Santa's work habits.

The next day, as Joe and I are reading the newspaper, he asks if I would accompany him on a walk around the block. "I try to walk for ten minutes each day," he tells me, folding his black reading glasses. "But I have to be careful when I'm walking alone. I tripped on a brick on the sidewalk last summer. I fell and broke my wrist."

"What if we go to the beach instead?" I suggest, setting my newspaper onto the coffee table. "I was going to drive Ben and Emma to the ocean, maybe walk awhile along the boardwalk. Why don't you come with us?"

"Yes, wonderful, wonderful, I would love to come." And he gets to his feet immediately, walking to the kitchen to tell Shirlee of the plan. He dons a pair of sunglasses and a cardigan sweater. Even though it's warm today, with temperatures in the high seventies, he wants protection from the sun and the ocean breeze.

I round up the kids and put the plan into motion.

"Can I bring my roller skates?" Emma asks as she slips into a pair of sandals, and I nod, looping the camera bag over my shoulder.

Ben pulls on a Florida Marlins cap. We call out our goodbyes to Cathy and Shirlee and walk out the door to the car in the driveway. Ben holds open the front door for Joe. Joe steadies himself, one hand on the door, and slides into the front seat.

I take a familiar route to the ocean, driving down a palm-lined boulevard past a strip mall, then crossing a bridge over the Intercoastal Waterway. Sunlight hits me in the face and I fish between the car seats for my Ray-Bans. Under the bridge, two jet skis shoot along the surface of the waterway as if they are about to take off and fly. I'd like to try that sometime, I think, but I keep it to myself. Ben, the junior environmentalist, would be all over my case if I admitted to such a politically incorrect day-dream.

I park the Thunderbird just off U.S. Highway A1A near the municipal pier at Deerfield Beach. Emma straps on her skates and rolls onto the pavement of the walkway.

"I'll pull you along," says Ben.

He takes Emma by the hand and tugs her down the oceanside promenade, dodging joggers and toddlers and young couples walking hand in hand. The walkway borders a public beach. Sand-caked kids in purple and pink bathing suits splash under outdoor showers as dads stand by with beach towels. Palm trees bow in the breeze. Seagulls squawk above our heads. A parasail glides high over the ocean blue. Waves are swelling to four or five feet, ideal for the legions of body surfers kicking in the water. I think of the sub-zero temperature back home in Milwaukee.

"It's a marvelous day," Joe says. He removes his sweater and I offer to carry it for him.

I enjoy his company. With my father long in his grave, I often feel robbed of any interaction with my father's generation of men, of older role models. At home at my local YMCA, a group of men in their seventies meets every Saturday morning for games of rac-quetball. I intentionally schedule my own Saturday workouts in the fitness room to coincide with their games, just to hear their locker-room banter. They come to keep fit, sure, driving their sturdy hearts to the limit before retiring to the steam room. But they also come to swap stories, to reminisce about jobs or wars or families. Occasionally, I strike up a conversation with one of them, usually about sports or the weather or some other mundane topic. It's only brief, but it's somehow satisfying to feel even dis-tantly related to these elders.

"Let's get something to drink," I suggest as we near the end of the walkway. "There's a place in this hotel up here that I've been to." The four of us cross the street and step up into a beach bar. An easterly breeze pours through the open windows as we claim a table.

"I want lemonade," Emma says. "Please."

"Me too, please," Ben says.

"All right, I'll have one too," I say. "What can I get for you, Joe?"

"I would like a glass of wine." I hesitate for a second before stepping to the bar to order. I know that Joe is forbidden by his doctor from drinking alcohol. His tolerance to alcohol has gotten extremely low as he's aged. Even wine, a staple in any Frenchman's diet, is taboo. But how can I deny a simple enjoyment to an eighty-nine-year-old man? I say to myself. What harm can one glass of wine do? I order Joe a Chardonnay.

"Thank you," he says, and the four of us clink our plastic glasses together. I feel as if we've granted Joe a furlough of some kind. He turns loquacious, the wine seeming to invigorate his memory. He begins to tell stories, evocative tales about growing up in France, stories of Hollywood, stories I've heard before but enjoy hearing again.

"I once made a movie in Africa, in Kenya. It was a movie about a safari, called *Hatari*. Howard Hawks directed the picture, and John Wayne and Red Buttons acted in it. It was a wonderful experience; there were animals everywhere we went, giraffes, zebras, antelope, beautiful, all of them. We shot several scenes with a rhinoceros bull running across the plain. We used Land Rovers—you've heard of them—with cameras fitted to the top. The script called for the rhinoceros to charge into a jeep and gore a passenger with its horn. It was very difficult, very dangerous for the actors."

"How long were you in Africa?" Ben asks, setting his glass on the table.

"I don't remember now exactly, it took months to shoot the picture. Halfway through the shooting, I contracted malaria. I was miserable, feverish all the time, even in the middle of the day. Terrible. But we kept shooting."

Ben and Emma listen in awe, captured by Grandpa Joe's tale, reveling in his companionship. It's unfair that they see their grandfather only once a year; it's unfair to him, too. All three of them relish this moment.

As the end of our vacation draws near, Ben and I decide to hit the highway. On each family visit to Florida, the two of us take off for a day or two on an exploration. It's become a custom. We pick a destination and just go.

One year, we went to the Everglades, where we rode a boat into the great mangrove swamp in search of alligators and manatees. The manatees stayed out of sight; the tidal creeks into the Glades were lousy with noisy tour boats. But driving along Alligator Alley on our way home, we stopped at a state hiking trail and came within yards of dozens of fat, smiling gators. From a wooden walkway, we watched spellbound as they drifted noiselessly in the swamp, stalking their prey.

A couple of years ago, during spring break, we traveled to a handful of major league training camps. At the Atlanta Braves camp in West Palm Beach, I had the chance to shake the hand of Henry Aaron, the hero of my boyhood Braves. In Fort Myers, we spent the day at the Minnesota Twins camp. For an afternoon game, we got seats behind the Twins dugout. During batting practice, first baseman Kent Hrbek, one of Ben's baseball champions at the time, ambled back to the dugout from the batter's box after cracking his bat. As he stepped off the field, Hrbek looked up at Ben in the stands. "Here you go, kid," he said, handing Ben his bat. Ben was the envy of every kid in the ballpark.

This time out, we've planned a day of snorkeling at John Pennekamp Coral Reef State Park, an underwater park in the Florida Keys. We'll sign up for a tour and spend the day at sea, mostly undersea, chasing fish.

In midmorning, we arrive on Key Largo, the first and largest island in the Keys. We roll past the hotels and restaurants without slowing and turn left off U.S. A1A into Pennekamp Park. The water in the distance is absolutely enticing, aquamarine, Caribbean.

It's a short walk to the visitor's center, where we buy two tickets for the 11 A.M. tour aboard the *El Capitan*. We have forty-five minutes before departure, enough time to rent our gear.

"This feels a little tight," Ben says, zipping the wet suit over his chest.

"It'll loosen up. When you're in the ocean, water collects between the wet suit and your skin. The water's warmed by your body and keeps you comfortable." I've snorkeled and scuba dived before, and undersea, even at ten feet, the water can be frigid.

Ben pulls a mask and snorkel over his face. "You look like an insect," I tell him. His nose is squeezed into the mask and the snorkel tube juts up like an antenna.

The *El Capitan* is a flat-bottomed boat that holds about fifty people. Most of the passengers are parents with children, kids as young as eight and nine. The boat lurches to a slow idle as we approach Banana Reef. Ben takes a sip from his plastic water bottle and then stows his backpack under the bench.

"Let's go for it," he says.

We take our place in line at the stern of the boat. Two crewmen are helping divers onto a wooden platform at the stern.

"You first, Dad."

I step onto a wooden platform and sit on the edge, dangling my feet above the water. I slide my mask over my face, slip my fins over my dive boots, give Ben a thumbs up, and jump.

I see nothing but white bubbles, swirling and dancing all around me. I float weightless as my inflated vest slowly returns me to the surface. I blow the water out of my snorkel, kick my fins, and swim forward, head down. Below, no more than thirty feet away, is the reef, a ridge of white sand, swaying plants, orange coral, and fish of every shape and size skirting away in every direction. I lift my head from the water just in time to see Ben pushing himself off the platform of the boat. He surfaces with a whale-blast of water from his snorkel and floats on his stomach, looking down. I swim to his side and tap him on the shoulder.

"Okay?" I ask. He spits out the mouthpiece, treading water.

"Okay. Yeah, okay." His bottom lip is quivering.

"Just relax. Don't wear yourself out. Stick close to me. Remember, rule number one: Swim with a buddy." He gives me a thumbs up. I bite down on my mouthpiece and we both dive under.

We glide along, a foot below the surface. The sky is cloudless and the seas are calm. We can make out shapes underwater from seventy feet away: long, dark, mysterious fish and thin, delicate sea fans the size of bedsheets. Sea grass on the reef dips and bends in the tide. A large fish with a dorsal fin gives us a start, and I'm relieved to see that it's a grouper and not a shark. But lurking near the sandy bottom is a school of barracuda, very real barracuda, five, six, seven of them, mean and menacing-looking. Everything appears larger than life underwater, and the barracuda look bigger than grown men, though I know they're probably no more than four feet long and more fearful of us than we are of them.

We steer clear of the barracuda and shoot to the surface to refill our lungs. It's like another planet under the ocean, a wonderland. For nearly an hour, we swim along the spine of the reef, careful not to touch the fragile, living rocklike organism.

A loud blast from the boat's horn signals that it's time to board. Ben and I are the last divers out of the water. We stumble back to our seats, our legs wobbly from the exertion, and the captain powers up the craft. We're on the way to Dry Rocks Reef, our second stop.

"I'm starving," Ben says, reaching for his backpack, not bothering to towel off. He rips open the wrapper of a granola bar.

"I think I saw a sea turtle," he says, shivering between bites. "On the bottom. In the sand. I thought it was a rock at first. But it moved."

We're soon submerged again, kicking on the surface, re-charged. By now Ben's a pro. He disappears beneath the waves, his fins driving him down, staying under for half a minute, then shooting up like a beluga, white water spraying from the blowhole of his snorkel.

Two other dive boats are anchored nearby, and a school of divers with tanks on their backs are floating in a congregation to our left. I had heard about an underwater tourist attraction out here, and I suspect this is the draw, so I wave at Ben to follow me. We swim for forty yards or so, then I give Ben a sign to dive. We vanish beneath the swells.

Underwater, set in the sand, standing on the reef, is a bronze statue of Christ, arms outstretched, eyes gazing up. Sea plumes sway in the tide current like deep-sea seraphs, brightly colored fish circle in a halo over the statue's head, scuba divers kneel and pray at its feet. Such a peculiar sight, a nine-foot statue, Christ of the Deep, balanced on the bottom of the ocean.

"How did that statue get there?" asks Ben, as we break the sur-face, the waves rocking us under a blue sky.

I raise my eyes upward, wide open, feigning astonishment. Ben grins, and we dive down for another look.

Three hours later, we're back on dry land. The western sky is a veil of purple and orange. It's dusk, and the "no-see-ums" are out in force, minuscule bugs, appropriately named, with a fondness for the tender skin on the back of a person's neck.

"Aayyyeeeeee!" Ben swats, spits, and wags his head madly. He races to the car, but it's locked. "Open it, open it," he pleads, and I run up from behind.

We polish off a couple of Burrito Supremes at a roadside Taco Bell and head back to Boca Raton, our excellent adventure com-plete. I swing the car onto A1A northbound and push the accelera-tor to the floor. I open my window and stick out my elbow. I've been down this highway before, a number of times with a number of people. I remember one trip with Cathy and a couple of our friends, before we had kids. We were coming off a week-long party in the Keys, speeding back to Miami International Airport in a rented convertible, probably listening to Jimmy Buffett on the tape deck. As I recall, someone had an open bottle of tequila in the back seat, and I would bet there were drugs in the car as well.

Today, I've got a bottle of premixed virgin piña colada between my knees as I drive, fruit juice and coconut milk. Buffett again is singing on the tape deck, but this time my traveling companion is my teenage son, who's drumming his hands on the car door, head out the window, checking the side of the highway for gators. It's funny how time can spin you in circles. The scenery is familiar, the luscious smells of these Florida Keys are the same, the tunes are identical. But the moment is so unlike the last time I was here. Act Two on the same stage.

"I was singing Jimmy Buffett while we were snorkeling," Ben confesses.

"Underwater?"

"Yeah. In my head, of course."

"Ben, Ben, Ben. You've crossed over. You've become a Parrothead."

We leave A1A and I turn onto a freeway ramp leading to the Florida Turnpike, the big silver Thunderbird flying across the pavement. The orange and purple has faded from the sky. Twilight and speed turns us pensive.

"Today was a good day," Ben says, contentedly. "Everything worked out, driving down here and everything."

"A smashing success," I say. "Just hunky dory."

"Hunky dory, yep. What does that mean, anyway? What is a *hunky dory?*"

"It means everything's all right, everything's just fine. It's a dumb cliché. Like, sitting on cloud nine. Or, in a pig's eye. Or, the cockles of your heart."

"So what's cockles?" he asks.

I give it some thought, then answer.

"Read between the lines," I say.

"Huh?"

"I'm pulling the wool over your eyes."

Now he gets it. "It's the blind leading the blind," he says.

"Chip off the old block," I return.

And he laughs. We've got a contest going, a road game to waste the time.

"Cool as a cucumber?" he tries.

"Dead as a doornail," I answer.

"Uh huh. Well, the squeaky wheel gets the grease."

"So don't make a mountain out of a molehill," I say. "You can be pretty good at that."

"I wasn't born yesterday."

"Or born with a silver spoon in your mouth."

"Not me."

"No, I guess not. So put your money where your mouth is."

We fly down the turnpike, silent now. "I'm stumped," Ben says. "I can't think of one."

"That's the way the ball bounces," I tell him, and we're rolling again, laughing.

"You've gotta sink or swim."

"Boys will be boys."

"Well, that goes without saying."

"Don't bite off more than you can chew."

"Don't cut off your nose to spite your face."

"Ooo, that's a good one," I say, but now *I'm* stuck, I've run out. I pause for a minute, then, finally: "I guess I'm left in the lurch, Ben."

"Ah ha. I guess the shoe's on the other foot, Dad."

"That goes without saying."

"Well, keep a stiff upper lip." And we laugh so hard I almost have to pull over to the side of the road.

* * *

Our Florida vacation ends on a somber note. Two days after Ben and I return from the Keys, Joe is admitted to the hospital. We had all decided to celebrate New Year's Eve by staying home—eating dinner and watching videos together at Shirlee and Joe's. Throughout the evening, as Shirlee, Cathy, and I were enjoying our wine, our vodka, our champagne—whatever was being poured—Joe had slyly and discreetly sampled each of our untended drinks, a sip here, a sip there.

The alcohol apparently was enough to do serious damage. In the middle of the night, Joe fell from his bed, incoherent, unable to stand. Throughout the night and into the morning, he grew more and more disoriented, speaking in French, unable to recognize his wife, his stepdaughter, his grandchildren, or me. Shirlee called the paramedics. After a series of tests, his doctor determined that he had suffered a small stroke, likely induced by the alcohol.

A day later, we visit Joe in his hospital room. Except for a security guard, the lobby is deserted. I punch the elevator button for the fifth floor.

Joe is propped up in his bed by two or three pillows, an IV line dangling from his arm. He appears small, tired. The light from the television casts the room in a greenish tint. The air smells stale, antiseptic.

"Hi, Grandpa," Ben says as we walk into Joe's room, trying to sound cheerful.

Emma is wide-eyed and silent. Joe smiles broadly, seeming to know us. But his mind is somewhere else.

"I won't be able to attend the party tonight," he tells us. "The costume party, it's downstairs. I can't go, I'm very sorry. But you must. You all must attend."

Cathy takes his hand. There is little to say. We make small talk, asking about the food, about the nursing staff. After fifteen minutes, we say good night and leave his room.

"I'll talk to you tomorrow, Joe," Shirlee says. "I'll give you a call in the morning."

But Joe shakes his head, confused.

As we file into the elevator, Emma is still mute. She is slowly losing the only grandpa she has known, and Ben, another male role model.

Joe was released from the hospital a week later. But his disorientation continued off and on, and his physical condition worsened. By the end of the month, he was admitted to a nursing home.

Our two-day drive home to Milwaukee is subdued. We read magazines, listen to book tapes, study the landscape. As we roll north, our Florida tans and sunny humor seem to fade by the hour. By the time we reach Wisconsin, the slate gray skies of winter have returned. We roll into our driveway and unload the car, chilled by the icy air yet glad to be home. My thoughts turn to Florida and to Joe, and I suddenly feel especially protective of my family, of my children, reminded how fragile life can be.

Birthdays

I have two vivid recollections of Ben's birth: Sunlight streaming through the hospital window minutes after he was born. And Dr. Julie's cowboy boots.

We were living in Colorado. Cathy was admitted to the hospital on a Monday night, the first of March, 1982. Snow had fallen during the day, a wet, heavy snow that cracks tree branches and triggers heart attacks but melts away in a day or two. I had been out listening to music at a local club that night, ostensibly gathering material for a music review I was assigned to write of some performer. I can't remember who, and the review was never written. Ben's debut took precedence.

I arrived home late from the bar, an hour before midnight. Those were the days before pagers and cell phones. Even though I was just minutes away, I was incommunicado when Cathy's water broke and her labor pains began. I paid the price.

"Where the hell have you been?" was Cathy's greeting as I walked in the back door of our flat. She stood listing in the hallway, one hand against the wall, one hand on her swollen belly, her chin dipped and her face in a grimace.

"But wait, you've got another two weeks before your due date," I stammered. "This isn't supposed to happen yet."

"This baby isn't waiting," she said. "It's coming. *Right now*."

I grabbed the suitcase she'd packed, and off we flew to the hospital.

Cathy was in labor all night long, huffing and puffing, scream-ing deliriously, waiting desperately for that kid to come OUT. I took my post beside her in the birthing room.

"Get away from me you son of a bitch! Your breath stinks! You smell like beer and coffee! How can you be so insensitive! You *bastard!*"

I did what I could. I poured drinking water. I fetched ice. I dimmed the lights. I brightened the lights. I guided Cathy to the toilet every four minutes, guided her into the shower so she could cool her overwrought body, guided her to the sink so she could throw up. Her most recent dinner had been *huevos rancheros*—green chile over fried eggs, a spicy dish that was dis-gorged by her body, à la Linda Blair, as projectile vomit. It's a messy process, birth, a liquid ordeal for all involved. Bodily flu-ids of every sort and color gush from all cavities of a mother and a newborn.

Cathy squatted, Cathy walked, Cathy paced the hospital room like a caged puma, making vows we both knew she'd never keep. "There is no way in hell I'll ever go through this again. I will never have sex again in my *life*. I will never, *ever* have sex with you . . . " Her pregnancy had been healthy and normal, but with all the attendant discomforts—the morning sickness, the sciatica, the waddling weight, the stomach-cramping insomnia. And now a pain like she had never known before.

Halfway through her labor, halfway through the night, I ducked out of the birthing room in search of another cup of cof-fee. In a corner of the hallway, lying sound asleep on a gurney and snoring comfortably as nurses and patients ambled by, was Dr. Julie Carpenter, our hippie obstetrician. A white sheet cov-ered all but the dark hair on her head and the black cowboy boots on her feet.

When the time finally came for the good doctor to go to work, Dr. Julie climbed off the gurney, adjusted her wire-rims, took her position at the foot of the bed, leaned back on her heels, grasped the baby's head, and pulled, firmly but gently. I focused on her boots, wishing I had a pair. Somehow they seemed like just the right shoes to wear to a birth.

"Here comes the head, okay," she said, digging in her heels. "I've got the head. Push more, Cathy, push a little harder, *harder*. Hooo! I see the shoulder, the shoulder's out, that's it, now take a deep breath and . . . push. Come on. *One more push.*"

I played no part in this triumph. All I could do was watch.

At 10:10 A.M., a baby popped out and opened his eyes for a look at life. The sun shone through a narrow window in the room, breaking through a snowy, overcast sky. The bald, pink-skinned baby fell asleep at Cathy's bosom, as she beamed and wept. We both beamed and wept, shivering in the magnitude of the day.

Later Cathy and I wrote a verse announcing the arrival.

With the early wet spring snows
And the late winter of '82 blues
Comes the first born baby boy
Benjamin Evan . . .
6 pounds, 3 ounces
And well worth the weight

Exactly fifteen years later, Ben has gained about a hundred pounds, a thick head of hair, a younger sister, and a welter of memories. New memories are born every day.

The evening of his birthday is gray and damp. Winter still holds us in its grip. But there's a springtime enthusiasm in the air. The temperatures are warming and the days are getting longer. A holiday spirit occupies our home. Birthday cards line the mantel above the fireplace, cards from Cathy's family in Florida and Boston, cards from friends in Minnesota and Colorado, cards from the Chandler family throughout Milwaukee. Emma herself has made a card for her big brother, a drawing in colored markers of a smiling pink face and a shining yellow sun. Boxes of gifts are stacked on the coffee table. A string of colored lights twinkles in the archway between the living room and dining room, still hanging from Christmas.

Ben and Emma sit on the floor face to face at the coffee table playing Candy Land.

"Emma, you little cheater," Ben complains, snickering. "You landed on the black dot, and you have to stay there until you get another yellow card."

"I *didn't*. I was on *purple*. I was *here*."

I won't referee. Let them settle it. I hunch over the piano, tinkering with the keys, trying to find a melody and chords. I don't play much. Cathy and I bought this old upright from neighbors years ago, pre-Ben, with money I had borrowed on a student loan. We've lugged it cross-country twice now, hoping the children will take an interest, and they have. Ben took lessons for years, still plays some, and Emma is learning with a play-by-colors lesson book. But on this evening of celebration, I'm the maestro. "Happy birthday"—the melody fills the air.

Cathy, meanwhile, is cooking Ben's favorite dinner: chicken *Française* with fettuccine alfredo, and chocolate mousse as his birthday cake. It's a menu to an adult's taste, no hotdogs and potato chips here. Thanks to the women in his family, Ben has a sophisticated palate. He'll still go for pizza or a burger, but he's more apt to order ethnic foods—Thai, Chinese, Mexican.

Cathy dishes out the fettuccine and calls us to the dining room.

"For your very first birthday dinner, Ben, we had Chinese takeout," she says as we sit. "We got an order of lo mein noodles. We sat you in your highchair, and you dug in with both hands and spread the noodles all over your face and in your hair. Bouncing up and down in your chair. We've got pictures somewhere."

Ben takes two helpings of chicken. The coming year will be a year of milestones, both big and small. In the spring, he will try out for the freshman golf and baseball teams. In three months, he'll finish his first year of high school. In summer, he'll begin the classroom session of driver's education, on the way to his learner's permit next fall. He'll no doubt complete other firsts in his life, feats and deeds that his parents will never know about.

Ben has other things on his mind. He puts down his fork.

"I was thinking of having a party here with my friends next Saturday night," he says. "Maybe have everyone sleep over."

"Well, sure, that's fine," says Cathy. "How many friends would you invite?"

"About five or six? We could rent a couple of videos and sleep on the floor."

"I can order pizza for dinner," Cathy says.

"That sounds good, Ben," I say. "I like your friends. And I'll do everything I can not to embarrass you."

"Thanks a lot, Dad."

Ben's birthday is turning into a weeklong event. On the coming Sunday, we'll invite my mother, my siblings, and their families for yet another round of celebration.

I can see that Emma is getting impatient with all this talk about her brother.

"When are we going to have cake?" she says, kicking her legs as they dangle under her chair.

We clear the table and I grab the camera. Cathy puts a match to fifteen candles on the chocolate mousse and carefully places the flaming dessert before Ben. I turn down the lights and focus my lens on Ben's grinning face.

Happy birthday to you, happy birthday to you . . .

"Make a wish, Ben," Emma reminds him. He thinks for a second and then blows out all the candles.

"What did you wish for?" asks Emma, clapping. But her question is blasphemous.

"If I tell you, I'll spoil it. It won't come true."

145

She's unconcerned. "On my birthday, I wished that Buttons would come alive," she says, and laughter lights the room.

Cathy cuts the cake and dishes the first slice to Ben. He guides a gigantic forkful to his mouth with his finger. She slices pieces for the rest of us. Emma goes silent, digging in.

"I like the chocolate mousse almost as much as your cheese-cake," I say. Cathy once ran a dessert company with a partner in Boulder. She lost money in the venture but left with some terrific recipes.

As Ben finishes his second slab of cake, I slide his birthday presents onto the table. He tears into the gift wrap, his sister helping, tossing paper around the room. Each box holds clothes: a pair of blue jeans, a black sweatshirt, a white T-shirt. And added to his teenage wardrobe is a pair of black leather boots, ankle high, laces up the front.

I lift one of the boots from the shoe box. "Are these Army issued? Steel-toed? Man, each shoe must weigh ten pounds. How are you going to walk in these things?"

Ben ignores me. He likes the boots. He's been hoping for a pair. He laces up both boots and clomps around the wooden floor and into the kitchen. The boots seem to enhance the slow, deep-heeled lope of his high school walk.

"With summer coming, why didn't you ask for a pair of deck shoes or something?" And I raise my foot in the air to model my own footwear.

"What, and look like you?"

As Ben models his new boots, I slip out the kitchen door and down into the basement for his last gift, his one big-ticket present this year. I return to the party and place a cardboard crate on the floor. It's unwrapped, and when Ben reads the printing on the side—20 INCH PORTABLE TV—his eyes grow wide.

"Hey, thanks. Thanks a lot."

"Open it, Ben," Emma says.

Ben pops the staples on the cardboard flaps and folds back the top.

With Ben's help, I pull the television set from the box and follow him into his bedroom. To make more room on his dresser, he pushes aside a couple of candles and a bottle filled with coins. I hoist up the new TV and plug it in.

We had reservations about buying Ben a television. Three TV sets in the house seems excessive. We try to limit our time in front of the tube. We've never had cable; the kids rarely complain. The set in Cathy's and my bedroom was a wedding gift. The family TV in the living room is used mostly for rented videos, a few select programs, and the news. But Ben's personal interests are separating from family interests. More and more, his room is becoming his refuge, a place to do his homework, listen to music, get away from his parents and sister if he wishes.

When I was growing up, my family never owned more than one TV set. When I was very young, it was an old Admiral console, a set with a fifteen-inch screen in a wooden cabinet with doors on the front. My brother Steve and I sat on the carpet three feet from the screen watching "The Howdy Doody Show" and "The Mickey Mouse Club." When I was about eight or nine, my parents replaced the Admiral with a black-and-white portable that could be wheeled on a stand from the living room to the kitchen during meals. Eventually we got a color set. I was sure I was the last of my friends to get color.

"The picture's a little fuzzy on channel twelve," I say as I adjust the antenna. "Try channel four. There, four's better."

The telephone rings.

"I bet I know who that is," says Ben. He hands me the remote and walks into the dining room. He picks up the phone and laughs, holding the receiver to his ear without speaking. His Grandma Shirlee in Florida has made her traditional call to sing "Happy Birthday" in her marvelously off-key voice.

"Thank you very much, Grandma," Ben says finally. "Yes, I got the boots. . . . Yep, they fit fine. I like them a lot. So does Dad . . ."

* * *

As he talks, I look around his bedroom, a foreign land to me most of the time. The room is small, cozy, filling fast with *stuff*. An ivy plant is draped along a bookshelf jammed with CDs, a dozen video cassettes of "The Simpsons" episodes, and books of all types—from Stephen King, Robert Heinlein, and a world atlas to a pictorial guide to one hundred and fifty years of baseball, *My Book About Me* by Dr. Seuss, and *Brave New World* by Aldous Huxley. A bulletin board is plastered with Ben's class schedule, a Canadian dollar bill, a bumper sticker from a radio station, and two or three political cartoons, one lampooning Barney, the purple TV dinosaur, who's being eaten by a tyrannosaurus in Jurassic Park. A NO PARKING sign hangs on a wall, a souvenir from I don't want to know where. A collection of old automobile license plates is tacked to his wooden door, and a framed photograph of the earth taken from space is mounted above his unmade bed. A half-eaten piece of aging pie sits on a plate on the nightstand, along with a milk-stained glass. A laundry basket overflows in one corner.

On the floor next to the laundry is a square wooden box. I've forgotten all about it. For Ben's first birthday, I had asked my father to build some sort of time capsule, leaving it up to him to design it. It was no surprise that he built a box made out of wood, his medium. Oak veneer, a foot high, a foot wide, a foot deep. He stained and varnished the box, inside and out, and put brass handles on two sides, adding a brass clasp for a small padlock. On the top, inset in the lid, he installed a surprise: a wind-up music chime that plays "Take Me Out to the Ballgame," salvaged from a music box he had found somewhere.

"Hey Ben, are you off the phone?" I call.

I give the music box a twist. It still works. Ben walks into the room and smiles when he hears the tune.

"What have you got in here?" I ask. "Take a look?"

"Open it. I hardly remember what's inside."

I sit on his bed and open the lid. The box is full of Ben's prized possessions, things he has collected over the years. On the top of the stack are baseball cards sealed in plastic: Kirby Puckett, Barry Bonds, Roger Clemens's rookie card, and dozens more. We dig deeper, archeologists sifting through newspaper clippings of World Series games we attended in Minnesota, a yearbook from Ben's grade school, awards he won for his work in a school play in middle school.

"You saved all this?" I say as I lay some of the treasures on his bed. "Old birthday cards, letters we mailed to you at summer camp, clay pottery you made in Cub Scouts, a silver dollar—"

My father shipped the finished wooden box from Wisconsin to our home in Colorado. Enclosed in the time capsule were two envelopes, one from my father and one from my mother, each addressed to Ben and sealed with the words "Do not open until your 10th birthday!"

The envelopes were opened by Ben exactly five years ago today.

My mother's envelope included a faded photographed of her hugging a fat-cheeked Ben at four months old, and another photo, me at ten years old, a fat-cheeked kid in glasses wearing a sport jacket and a tie. And a letter:

February 24, 1983

Dearest Ben,

When you open this on your tenth birthday, you will be in fifth grade in the year of 1992. One can wonder what you will be studying in school. We are on the threshold of the computer age now and in 1992 it will probably be "old hat." I hope by then the world will have settled its differences and learned to live in peace.
Well dear, I wish you all the health and happiness in the world.

Your loving Grandma Rose

* * *

The second envelope, addressed to "Master Ben Chandler," was written in my father's hand:

Feb. 26, 1983

To Grandson:

Today is your 10th birthday and you have opened the time capsule that your Mom & Dad made up for you nine years ago.

I hope you enjoy this and have many questions to ask about its contents. Grandma and I hope we are with you when the capsule is opened so we also may enjoy your day.

I've sent you ten dimes of old silver, one for each of your years. I hope you enjoy them.

Lots of love,
Grandpa Kent

Stuffed inside the envelope is a photograph of my father and baby Ben, laughing at each other, their faces inches apart, and taped in rows to the back of the photo are ten Liberty Head dimes.

"This is priceless," I say quietly. "Don't ever lose this."

Emma climbs onto the sofa between Cathy and Ben. Ben is paging through a family photo album. It's late in the evening. The hours of his fifteenth birthday are running out.

"Oh God, I remember this," says Cathy, pointing to a photo. There's a close-up of Ben as an infant nestled under his young mother's chin, both of them asleep. There's another picture of Ben sitting naked in the bathtub, a dripping washcloth in his mouth.

There's a picture of Ben smiling devilishly at the camera as he pulls his clothes from a dresser drawer.

"Old habits die hard," I say, and Ben wrinkles his face at me.

"Do you recognize yourself in that little boy?" I ask him. "Is that still you?" He stares at his countenance and shrugs indifferently.

He can't see it, but I know it's the same boy, the same Ben there. Even though he now shaves nearly once a week and works hard to master the perfect teenage glower, he's the same bright and playful and inquisitive kid he was so long ago, the boy who insisted upon having a book read to him every night, who laughed hysterically when he ran his oatmeal-coated hands in his father's beard, who chased the cats around and around the coffee table and bounced balloons off the ceiling fan.

"I miss that little boy sometimes," Cathy confesses.

"Get over it, Mom," Ben groans.

"Never," she says, and turns the page.

"Where was this taken?" Ben asks, looking at yet another image of himself.

"Let me see," and I slide next to him on the sofa. It's a picture of Ben at four years old. He's wearing a bright rainbow-colored shirt and walking along a dirt road in the mountains, a roaring waterfall behind him. I took the photograph, but it's an image not happily remembered.

It was a crisp, sunny summer day, and Ben and I went on a hike near a small mountain town named Caribou. We rambled along a dirt road through the pines and aspen with no destination in mind, and then suddenly the wind kicked up from the west, bringing an afternoon shower with it. I had stuffed my backpack with animal crackers, apple juice, and a red Mickey Mouse sweatshirt, but I wasn't prepared for rain. I scooped Ben into my arms and began jogging back to the car. And as we passed a wooden A-frame cabin along the side of the road, an older couple called out from their front porch.

"Come in, come in," they waved.

The couple introduced themselves as Carl and Martha. Carl was an engineer, Martha a retired science teacher. They lived in Denver and retreated to their mountain hideout nearly every weekend. A wood-burning stove warmed the cabin. A vase of wildflowers sat on a bare wood table in the center of the room. Martha heated water for hot chocolate and tea, and as we sat, Carl placed a wooden crate filled with toys in front of Ben.

"These are for our grandchildren when they come up to visit," he said. "We've got two granddaughters and one grandson, just about that fella's age."

We traded small talk and watched as Ben scattered Matchbox cars in every direction across the floor. In a short time, the rain let up and the sun returned, gleaming through a window. Ben and I went on our way, thanking the two for their hospitality.

"Tank yoooo," Ben sang out as we continued our hike, and the couple returned to their high-backed wooden rocking chairs on the porch, hand in hand after the summer rain.

That image of Carl and Martha on their porch is still painful. It was so incongruous with my own life then. Cathy and I had been separated for a month. I had moved in with mutual friends, convinced that the relationship was over. A few months earlier, I had started working as a reporter at a small newspaper. The enthusiasm of starting a new career had collided with the insecurities of fatherhood and what I saw as a lackluster marriage. Cathy was working part-time in a ski factory while providing the lion's share of care for Benjamin. She was envious of my new life, yet unable (or unwilling, as I believed then) to do much with her own. Our relationship had become a grudge match over our individual needs, and our arguments had become stormy repeat performances, never with resolution.

"What would you like me to do?" Cathy would plead. "Apparently I can't be the person *you* want me to be."

"I want you to be the person you want to be," I'd reply.

"But you don't like that person."

"That's not true, *you're* the one dissatisfied with your life."

And around and around we'd go.

Maybe it's time to move on, I thought, but move on to what? I didn't know. It seemed easier to look back than ahead. I spent most of my evenings sitting in the backyard of my friends' home, staring into an empty field or reading. Cathy and I would talk on the telephone, and we would admit that we missed each other, but as soon as we tried to figure out ways to shake loose of our limbo, the cross-analyzing would begin and we'd return to our grudge match.

During the separation, someone gave me a book, *Dale Loves Sophie to Death*, by Robb Forman Dew. It was a novel about the failings and triumphs of a contemporary marriage, very frank, very personal. At one point in the book, the husband is attracted to another woman, a woman named Claire. At the end of the chapter, I found these words:

> When he looked at Claire and poured more wine, he discovered that his desire had dissipated, that he felt instead overwhelmingly depressed, with a longing for his own home, his own wife, his own children. He had a heartsick need for that quiet and continual celebration of the spirit when it is bound fast by the expectations and wants and demands of other people whom one desires above all else to please and cherish and be nurtured by in turn.

After three months, I moved back home. Cathy and I began counseling, began to rebuild our relationship, each of us agreeing to slip into each other's shoes as we could and into each other's arms as we desired.

On weekends, Cathy, Ben, and I returned to taking long hikes in the mountains, and I basked in that "quiet and continual celebration of the spirit" of my wife and son. Sometimes we would walk down that same dirt road where Ben and I had hiked. And sometimes we would get caught in a rain shower.

The camera is balanced on a tripod in the middle of the living room for one last photo, a family pose, the four of us together. I set the timer, push the shutter button, and dash into the frame, counting—"six, five, four, three . . . " I take my place next to Cathy on the couch and squeeze her hand.

The strobe flashes and the moment is preserved.

"Okay, one final tradition," I say, and I queue up a song on the CD player. It's a cut from the Beatles' *White Album*, a song I play on birthdays whenever I can get away with it. The CD drops into place and I push the play button. Ringo's drums explode, the rest of the Fab Four join in with a burst of noise, and Cathy begins to sing. "You say it's your birthday . . ."

"Nooooooo!" yells Ben. Evidently, two off-key voices on the same night—both carrying part of his genetic makeup—are too much to take. He flees the living room, hands over his ears.

The following Saturday, Ben organizes the sleep-over party at our home, a belated birthday bash. He invites four boys and two girls—four young men and two young women, really, two young women who will *not* be sleeping over.

Before the party begins, I volunteer to drive Ben and three of his buddies to the video store to pick out a couple of movies.

"Let's take the Subaru," I say, and we walk outside. As the boys climb into the back seat, I hear someone snickering.

"Ah, Mr. Chandler," says Dan, "I see you don't use a key to start this car."

Ben laughs, slightly embarrassed.

"Don't need one," I reply, holding the ignition in my fingers. It dangles by a wire beneath the steering column. "I've got a screwdriver to start it." I insert a screwdriver into the ignition and give it a turn. The car starts right up.

"No turn signals either," Ben notes. "But it's got a better radio than in Mom's car," he adds, defending me, or perhaps the Subaru.

It may be time to allow this rolling heap to give up the ghost. Once a rugged and reliable four-wheel-drive wagon, the 1983 Subaru has seen better days. The blue exterior is splotched with red primer, covering the rust spots. The hood has to be pried open with a crowbar. The rear windshield wiper is missing, and there is a gaping hole in the floorboard on the driver's side, big enough to see through to the pavement. I won't drive the car on the highway with a passenger for fear of a crash. Who knows, a front wheel might pop off or the whole car could burst into flames.

Maybe it's time to shop around for a new ride, I tell myself. Even Ben's friends are hinting.

"Ah, Dad, you were supposed to turn there," Ben says on the short drive to the video store.

"Oh, yeah. Missed it." I wag my head to clear my thoughts and take the next left.

"You're losing it, Dad," he says.

"Maybe, maybe. It happens, you know."

We reach the store and the boys pile out. I follow them inside. They've already zeroed in on two aisles, searching for movies labeled either Action or Horror.

"How about *Texas Chainsaw Massacre*?" says Dan. "We gotta get it if it's in."

"I've seen it about eight times," says Pete, studying the cover of a tape titled *Sexual Outlaws*, featuring an actress with ample cleavage.

"*Twister*?" someone says.

"Saw it."

"*Alien 3*?"

"Saw it."

155

"*True Lies?*"

"I can't stand Arrrnold."

"Here, look at this," Ben says. "*Puppet Master 4.* I've seen *Puppet Master 2* and *3.* They were great."

"Let's see the cover," says Brian, and they give it a look.

"Yeah, take it. Sure. Definitely." Four thumbs up. "Now, what else?"

I search the rack for movies I've seen, trying to be helpful.

"How about *Misery?*" I offer. "That was pretty good, pretty creepy. Or maybe something with Johnny Depp? He's good."

But no one is listening. They've got their own tastes, their own minds to make up.

They move down the aisle, shuffling along the green carpet as a clot of blue jeans and flannel, oblivious to anyone else around them. I follow behind at a distance, hands in the pockets of my leather jacket, baseball cap on my head, the overseer, the old fart, but not minding at all. Ben stands three or four inches shorter than each of his buddies, even with his new boots on, but he's lost all self-consciousness about his height. These days he's more interested in the sound of his own voice, questioning, testing conventions, risking opinions.

During parent-teacher conferences a month ago, each of Ben's teachers had strong opinions about *him.* His speech teacher described him as "intense" and "motivated," descriptions that Cathy and I have heard for years. "He's an amazing kid," said his math teacher, causing Cathy to blush with pride. "Out of all my classes," he added, "he's my favorite freshman."

Ben's grades have been good, mostly A's so far. Not only are his teachers pushing him to do his best, but—I was pleased to hear—he was pushing them back.

"Ben can be a real challenge sometimes," his art teacher conceded, and his history teacher summed him up this way: "Ben likes to push people's buttons. By his junior year, he'll be a real piece of work." I saw the prediction as a compliment.

We've been in the video store fifteen minutes, and the boys still haven't found two movies that they can agree on. This is a tough task, finding common ground among four teenagers.

"Hey, let's get *Taxi Driver*," Ben tries, plucking De Niro from the rack.

"No, no," I interrupt. "Find something else."

"Come on, Dad. I've seen R-rated movies before."

"Not this one. There are some very intense scenes in that movie, some very adult scenes. Try something else."

He gives up without much of a fight, knowing he can't win this argument. After all, I have the cash and the car keys. Er . . . the screwdriver.

Finally, the boys reach a consensus. They settle on *Puppet Master 4* and *Jason Goes to Hell: The Final Friday*.

"Two excellent choices, gentlemen," I say as we wait in the checkout line.

"I think so too," smiles Dan.

When we get home, Cathy is setting snack food on the dining room table, bowls of pretzels, potato chips, taco chips, picante sauce and guacamole, and bottles of root beer.

"I ordered two pizzas, one veggie, one pepperoni," she says.

For dessert, there's a gallon of frozen custard, a Wisconsin favorite. It's a junk-food feast.

There's a knock on the front door. Ben grabs a handful of pretzels and lets in his friend Chris and the two invited girls, Laura and Karla. The girls take a seat next to each other on the floor. Laura has a point-and-shoot camera and takes a picture of Ben, the birthday host. Ben mugs for the camera, tossing a taco chip at Pete, who tries unsuccessfully to catch it in his mouth—an action shot. After four or five tries (and a half-roll of film) they finally make the shot, to the sound of thunderous applause. Ben loads CDs into the player. One boy dances, playing air guitar. A couple of other boys cluster at the computer playing an adventure game, and suddenly the house is filled with a crowd of teens, laughing, raising their voices above the music, trying to outshout each other, outshine each other as they tell their stories of new discoveries, new observations, brainstorms from the blustery minds of adolescents.

"What if, like, we all showed up at school Monday with a tattoo of Bart Simpson on our arms?" Ben says, and they break into cheers.

Cathy rolls her eyes and retreats to the kitchen. I'm right behind her. Emma remains, sitting in the center of the living room, wrapped in awe and envy. Older kids are pure entertainment for her, real-life sitcom, better than anything on TV.

Cathy and I eat dinner in the kitchen with Emma while the teens gather in the dining room, heaping pizza onto paper plates.

"Why can't I eat with Ben and his friends?" she frowns.

"It's your brother's party, Sweets," Cathy explains. "I think you should give him and his guests some privacy."

As I take a bite of vegetarian pizza, a loud thud comes from the living room followed by hooting from the girls. Casually, I step around the corner to see what has caused the ruckus. On the living room rug are Pete and Brian, wrestling. Pete has Brian pinned on his back, and both boys are laughing, their faces bright red. Laura is taking snapshots of this over-aggressive male behavior, giggling as the camera flashes.

Ben looks my way and tries to stop the wrestlers. "Knock it off, you guys."

I plant myself on the piano stool for a few minutes with my paper plate on my knee, purposely making my presence known, a reminder to them that they *are* being supervised, that they *are* guests and must behave accordingly. The boys return the coffee table to its original position and the wrestlers return to their corners, laughing, panting, a bit flustered.

Cathy puts Emma to bed and retires to our bedroom to read. I decide to put in some time at work in my basement office. I tramp down the steps, close my office door, and sit at the keyboard, listening to the music and the laughter above. The racket soon dies down. I climb the stairs to check on the party. All but one lamp is turned out in the living room, and a videotape is rolling in the VCR, *Jason Goes to Hell*, I believe, judging by the guy in the mask. The silence is broken by periodic screams and laughter, as one ludicrous fright scene follows the next.

The movie ends in a hush, and Karla calls her father for a ride home. It's after midnight.

"Happy birthday, Ben," the girls sing out as Ben opens the front door for them. "Thanks for the party. See you guys at school on Monday," and out they go.

It's late, the pizza is devoured, the wrestling match is over, and the five boys sack out on the couch and the floor in their sleeping bags. Ben shoves *Puppet Master 4* into the VCR and switches off the last burning light. They watch in darkness, hypnotized by the TV screen, wiped out on junk food and root beer. The perfect birthday party.

Spring Training

I return home from the YMCA late on a Wednesday afternoon after a long workout on the exercise machines. Along with my day-to-day middle-age vanity, a strong motivation for toning up has been one simple, daily duty: carrying my kindergarten daughter without straining myself. Each school day at 7 A.M., it is my duty and joy to hoist lazybones Emma from her bed and carry her downstairs to the living room sofa. For that short morning minute, I am the Daddy of All Titans, and not some thin-haired guy with a bad lower back.

I park my car at the curb in front of our house and jog up the front steps and onto the porch, gym bag slung over my shoulder. As I fumble for my keys, I see Cathy through the glass of the front door, waiting.

"You know, if I get to the Y twice a week, my back pains disappear," I tell her, coming through the door. "I haven't seen the chiropractor for months."

But I see that Cathy's not interested in my lower back. Her face is filled with worry, a mother's worry. I've seen it before: jaw set, teeth clenched, stare fixed, the lines at the corners of her eyes deepening.

"Listen," she says. "Ben came home from golf practice in tears. He broke his new golf club. I don't know how. He wrapped it around a tree or something. But he hasn't come out of his room since he walked in. He's afraid you're going to be furious. And disappointed with him."

I set down my gym bag, take off my cap, and hang my jacket on a coat tree in the hallway. I'm feeling too good to be furious. It's spring, the grass is green again, leaves are bursting to life, daffodils are blooming, the neighborhood is lush and alive with the sounds of songbirds and the smell of sweetness, of fertility. Even my back feels good. How can I be furious?

"The putter? He broke the putter?"

"He said it's ruined," Cathy answers. "He won't talk to me about it."

I bought him a new putter as a Christmas present. It wasn't a terrifically expensive golf club, but I *am* disappointed. What disturbs me more, though, is the expectation that I will be furious, an expectation that I am forever trying to live down.

I take a breath and knock on the door to Ben's bedroom. He's lying in bed, fully clothed, his shoes still on his feet, his head under the quilt. The putter lies on the carpet in the center of the room. In two pieces. The head of the club is snapped off clean.

"What happened, Ben? How did you break it?" I stand in the doorway, hands at my side, trying to keep the tone of my voice agreeable.

"I threw it," he says, speaking through the blue quilt.

"It looks like you threw it hard. Why?"

"I don't *know* why," he says, a slight quiver in his voice.

But I know. His anger, the male anger, had flared up again. His hormones had redlined. He is thrown into these dark moods more and more as he moves toward adulthood. It's a side of him that rarely surfaced when he was a child.

"What set you off?"

I sit on the foot of his bed. He lies motionless for a second, and then he lifts the quilt from his face. His eyes are red.

"I couldn't golf today," he says. "I sucked."

"So you threw your putter into the air—"

"—and it broke when it hit the ground," he finishes the sentence.

Golf isn't supposed to be a contact sport. Anger doesn't mix well with the gentlemanly game; it almost never helps your score.

"One reason for you joining the golf team was to learn sportsmanship," I tell him. "Sending your golf club sailing through the air is hardly good sportsmanship. It's reckless. Something a knucklehead would do."

"I know, I know, I just lost it."

I try to keep my lecture short and to the point. "You can't let your anger get the best of you. You've got to work at it, work to control it. Like controlling your slice."

He pulls the covers over his head again.

"As I've said before, Ben, there are always consequences for our actions. Sometimes good, sometimes bad. In this case, the consequences are going to be bad: You'll have to buy a new putter by saving up your allowance. And until you do, you'll have to use that old putter you've got."

"It doesn't matter," he says. "I'm not going to play golf anymore. I got cut from the team."

"What? For throwing your putter?" It seems kind of unjust.

"Because I *stink*," he says. "My scores are really bad."

"Sorry to hear that," I say. He played in only one tournament and he played badly. He never got a chance to redeem himself.

"All you can do is do your best. You'll try again next year."

"I suck," he concludes.

"Don't beat yourself up over this," I say. "You're not the first person to get cut from the golf team. And you're not the first person to get angry on a golf course. People have committed murder on golf courses. Golf clubs get tossed and golf clubs get broken. Learn from this, think about it, and let it go. You'll get another chance next year."

I pick up the golf club to inspect the damage and lay it back down onto the floor. I shake Ben's leg under his covers.

"Get out of bed, Ben. Wash your face. Try to shake it off."

It's times like these when the complications of adolescence make me wish Ben was seven again. Raising a kid in the single digits is so much easier.

Ben's run of bad luck is not over. The following day, he arrives home from school, slams the door, drops his backpack on the floor, gives it a kick, and sinks into the sofa.

"I blew my math test," he says, worry and disappointment creasing his young forehead. "Got a fifty-three. There goes any chance I had of acing math this semester. I'll probably get a C now."

I'm sitting at the computer in the other room with a cup of lukewarm coffee at my side. But I see that my work will have to wait. I lift the coffee cup from the desk and myself from the chair and move into the living room.

"Why don't you see how you do on your final exam before you throw in the towel," I say to Ben. But he's not in the mood for fatherly advice.

"And I also found out that baseball tryouts start next week." He rubs the palms of his hands over his eyes, trying to rub away the stress. "I haven't had any time to practice, and you've been too busy. I'm not going to make the team."

I won't be drawn into the guilt trap. "Ben, you're too young to be stressed out," I say. "We'll get some practice in, don't worry. Let me be the one responsible for worrying, okay? It's my job." Self-doubt, anxiety, dread. These are adult traits, not a teenager's.

"Remember last summer," I try. "Remember that storm we got caught in?"

We had been camping on the East Coast, at Assateague Island National Seashore, a sandy barrier island off Maryland. It was a beautiful place, no traffic, no tourists. A herd of wild ponies ran free along the dunes. On our second day camping, we spent the morning on the beach, body surfing and reading. In the afternoon, the wind shifted and the sky turned slate gray. By early evening, a huge bank of thunderheads had formed to the west, blotting out the sunset like India ink. As night fell, lightning cracked on the horizon and thunder rumbled across the flat island. Our radio warned of a storm that had tumbled trees and power lines in Washington and Baltimore earlier in the day. Now it was heading out to sea. We sat on the crest of a dune near our campsite and watched it approach.

"Can't do much about it," I said to Ben. "Let's load some of our gear into the trunk of the car, just to be safe."

The rain hit at nine o'clock, falling sideways. We retreated to our tent. From inside we saw that the wind was ripping the tent stakes from the sand.

"We need something to hold this thing down!" I shouted.

"How about a few rocks from the campfire?" Ben said.

We scrambled around the campsite, lightning flashing, wind and rain pelting us. After filling the tent with as much ballast as we could find, we raced to our car, drenched from our hats to our shoes.

"Let's wait it out," I said, slamming the car door. Rivulets of water poured down all around us. Gusts of wind rocked the car back and forth.

"It feels like we're in a car wash," said Ben.

We watched through the steamed glass of the car, trying to tune the radio to a weather report but with no luck.

An hour later, the rain ended and the wind subsided. The damage had been done. We returned to our campsite and saw our tent folded over a wire fence like a downed kite. The canvas fly was torn and it was soaked with water, inside and out, uninhabitable for the night.

"Now what are we going to do?" said Ben.

"Looks like we'll have to sleep in the car," I said. "It's not that bad. It could've been worse."

We spread out the tent to dry and went back to our car. As we stretched out in the bucket seats in our rented Pontiac, the sky cleared and the stars reappeared. Through the windshield, the vast Atlantic loomed in the distance, breakers crashing along the shore. I cracked open a window, and the sound of the sea lulled us to sleep.

We woke at dawn and stepped out of the car. The birds sang, the sun rose in the eastern sky, the air warmed, and our eyes were filled with the light of a new day.

"Each day is different," I now say to Ben, sitting next to him on the sofa. "Some days will eat you up and spit you out for no good reason at all, and others will be pure joy, as easy to take as a sunny day in June. You've got to learn to ride out the bad ones. I'm still learning that too. Or, here, try the baseball analogy: Ty Cobb had a lifetime batting average of .367—one of the best ever. When you do the math, that means he got a hit for every three times at bat. Life's daily success rate is about the same. You just can't get on base every time you're up to bat."

He lifts his chin and looks pensively at me for a second, and I think he understands.

A few days later, I walk into the dining room and see that the red light is flashing and flashing and *flashing* on the answering machine. "Am I the only one who ever checks the damn phone messages in this house?" I gripe out loud to no one in particular.

I punch the button on the machine and listen. The message is a gift, a gift to me: "Hello, this is a call for Kurt," comes a woman's voice. "I'm calling from the Wisconsin Composers Circle to congratulate you on winning our songwriting contest. Your song won first place in the folk-song category. I'll call you tomorrow with the details, Kurt."

"What was that all about?" Ben says, listening from the living room.

"Sounds like I won a songwriting contest," I say, astonished. "I entered last fall, sent in a few tapes and forgot all about it. Who woulda thunk it?"

"Congratulations," he says, and walks into the dining room to show he means it. "Hey, that's great, Dad."

"It is, isn't it."

Life can be so unpredictable. Just weeks ago, things seemed so dark and doubtful. I was wrapped up in myself, worried about the future, wishing I was young again and could do it all over, or deciding I was an old man, done with ambition. You throw up your hands in frustration and think it's time to find a simple job working outdoors or something when, out of the blue, good fortune knocks at your back door.

Life has been on the upswing lately, but I won't be fooled into thinking it will always be this way. There will be another downturn, I'm sure, followed by another upswing, up and down. Still, I'm learning to enjoy the good times when they arrive.

I take my guitar from its stand in the corner of the room and start to play.

It's a clear Saturday morning. The air is cool and fresh, the humidity is low, a slight breeze blows from the south. It's perfect weather for baseball, for shagging flies, for hitting fungoes, for turning a couple of sweet double plays on a dirt infield.

Ben and I deliver Emma to a friend's birthday party, then drive to a nearby city park. There are five baseball diamonds in the park, good diamonds, well groomed. I pull into an empty parking lot.

"Looks like we've got the place all to ourselves," I say, and open the back hatch of my station wagon to gather our equipment. Ben sits on the bumper and changes into a pair of cleats.

"Still fit?" I ask.

"They're tight," and he kicks his heels on the asphalt. "I'm going to have to look for another pair."

"I should get a new glove," I say, yanking at the rawhide laces of my mitt. It's an infielder's mitt, an off-brand Eddie Matthews PLAY OK model (which pretty much sums up my ability as an infielder). I got it as a gift from my parents when I was a boy. I treasured the glove, oiled and massaged the leather every day, tied a hardball inside with rawhide to form a perfect pocket. Now it's worn out, used up. The laces have torn away from the webbing. The strap over the back of my left hand is frayed. The Eddie Matthews signature burned into the leather is barely legible, although I can still make out my own name, written with blue marker on the thumb so many years ago.

Ben's mitt is new, a Wilson, well made; no player's signature burned into the leather, though. It's an infielder's mitt with a strap over the back of the hand that's loosened and tightened with Velcro. Ben has played on Little League teams since he was eight. He usually plays infield—second base or shortstop; occasionally he's shifted to the outfield.

I crease the visor of my baseball cap, an orange-and-gray San Francisco Giants cap, a souvenir from a game I was at long ago in Candlestick Park.

"Keith is going to meet us here," I say as Ben ties his laces. "Let's toss the ball around until he shows up."

Keith and I have known each since early in high school. We've traveled together, followed each other's paths through life, celebrated each other's triumphs, mourned each other's losses. We have figured out the problems of the world so many times, on so many smoky, drunken nights, that we each could qualify for a seat in the United Nations. When we were in our early twenties, I persuaded him to move to Colorado after I had moved there, and when we were in our early forties, he lured me from Minnesota back home to Wisconsin, after moving home himself, by way of

St. Louis and Santa Cruz. He lives in the city with his wife, Pattie.
The four of us often go out together, to dinner, plays, parties, and
movies.

Keith is a good talker, a critical thinker, outspoken, never afraid
to tell people what he thinks. I can be the same way, and that has
led to trouble sometimes. When the two of us are together in a
group of people, we work a little too hard at playing the antago-
nists. We've offended many a friend and stranger over the years,
and argued fiercely with each other plenty of times as well, yet
we've always managed to repair the breach before any lasting damage to our friendship occurred. At a party once, the two of us went
nose to nose about something forgettable, coming close to blows
and sending guests running for the kitchen. One man, though, a
man from Italy, relished the noisy quarrel. "Yes, yes, this reminds
me of being home," he said to the host, laughing. "They argue so
passionately, they must be Italian."

Keith has watched Ben grow up; he knows him like an uncle.
Maybe better.

A car rolls into the lot and stops. Keith steps out and throws his
baseball glove at Ben.

"Benny boy! How are you?"

Ben catches it and throws it back.

"Hi, Keith. Good to see you."

"Hey, bud," I say to him, "ready for spring training?"

We shake hands. "So what's new?" I ask.

"Ah, well, let's see, my hair's growing back and my pecker's getting longer," he says, smiling.

"How is that possible?" I say. "I mean, the part about your hair
growing back."

Ben hides a grin and takes a wooden bat from the back of the car.

"Let's take this open diamond over here," I say, and lead Ben
and Keith to the infield, carrying three hardballs in my glove.

"So you're trying out for the freshman team?" asks Keith.
"When do tryouts start?"

"Tuesday," says Ben.

"You need to get in shape fast," Keith says. "Come on, three laps around the field."

We drop our gloves and break into a run, kicking up dust as we race for the bases. But Keith and I quickly give up the lead to Ben and jog leisurely around the diamond.

"No use wearing ourselves out right away," says Keith.

We finish our laps and then play three-man catch, loosening our arms, stretching our muscles. I lob the ball to Keith at first base, Keith lobs it over to Ben, and Ben sends it back to me, up into the blue and down into a glove, a steady cadence, so habitual, meditative. What could be more satisfying?

When I was a boy, my father and I would retreat to the backyard after dinner every evening for some catch, beginning in the soggy month of April. My father's mitt was dark leather, the color of old motor oil, and when it wasn't on his hand, it was as flat as a couch cushion, with about as much shape. He had found it, he said, when he was a kid, and never had the desire (or disposable income) to buy a replacement. But it served the purpose. The two of us would stand on opposite ends of the wide backyard, and he would throw that ball to me (*at* me) as hard as he could, as straight as a telephone wire. I would try to do the same. Back and forth we would throw, neither of us saying a word, an invisible line connecting my father's hand to mine, my hand to his, back and forth, ball meeting leather, slapping out a rhythm, a pulse. He would bounce a grounder to my left, to my right, or heave it high into the sky, higher than I'd ever seen a ball thrown, until I could barely see its outline against the dimming sky.

My father coached my Little League team for a couple of years, and I became the starting third baseman. I was, after all, the coach's son. I confess I wasn't much of a hitter, but I could peg the ball from corner to corner whenever it was hit my way. Once, when I was about twelve, the team was taking batting

169

practice. The sun was going down at Lion's Park. Charlie, our ace pitcher, was throwing heat from the mound, and my father was standing behind the catcher, foolishly not wearing a face mask, checking Charlie's control. Apparently Charlie's control was off the mark. One of his fastballs blew past the catcher's mitt and—whock!—hit my father square in the nose. He stomped around in circles behind home plate. I had rarely seen him in such pain.

"Goddamn it!" he cried, his hand shaking as he squeezed his nose between a finger and a thumb. "Goddamn it, goddamn it, god*damn* it!" The flurry of unspeakables seemed to stop the bleeding.

Charlie and the rest of us gathered around my father, unsure what to do.

"Geez, I'm sorry, Mr. Chandler," said Charlie. "You okay? Geez, I'm sorry. Geez."

But I didn't buy his sympathy. Charlie was a brute of a kid, tall, with sandy blond hair, dull gray eyes, and dark sideburns growing on his long face far too soon for a kid his age. When his fastball had met my father's nose, I had seen Charlie grin. Just for an instant, hiding his wretched face behind his glove. I hated him for that.

Practice was over. My father drove straight to the nearest hospital. Calmly and stoically, he held the steering wheel with one hand and a red-stained handkerchief to his nose with the other, instructing me to shift the gears as we rode. I later overheard him telling my mother how painful the broken nose was, but he never mentioned the pain to me.

My father's nose healed without any noticeable crook. A year or two later, as I reached my teenage years, rebellion took hold, and I stopped playing and he gave up coaching. Without much notice by either of us, those one-on-one evenings in the backyard came to an end.

Ben starts to burn 'em in, throwing hard and fast from third base to me at the plate. I dance away as one of his throws hits the dirt, protecting myself with my mitt as the ball skates past.

"You're going to throw out your arm, slow it down," I yell over my shoulder as I chase after the ball.

"Let's try a little infield practice," I shout. "Ben, take second. Keith, why don't you cover first and I'll hit some grounders. Ben, make the play to first."

Ben crouches, hands on knees, balancing on the balls of his feet. He pounds the pocket of his glove, shifting his weight from side to side, his blue cap shielding his eyes from the sun. I throw the ball up, twist my waist, and swing the bat. The ball flies over the pitcher's mound and skims off the infield grass toward the second-base bag. Ben is fast off his feet. He backhands the grounder with his glove, spins in the dirt, and throws, and the ball soars over Keith's head, out of his reach and into a chain-link fence. Keith turns and tracks down the errant baseball.

"Whoa, there!" I shout to Ben. "Easy does it. And Keith, man, you've got to get up for those. You could've had that."

"Twenty years ago, maybe," he grins. "Not today." He flips the ball back to me at home plate.

We try it again, Ben alert, poised, Keith watchful too, engaged in the moment. I rest the bat on my shoulder, dig my feet into the brown dirt, focus my eyes ahead, toss the ball with my left hand, and swing. A simple movement, so it seems, and that's the beauty of baseball, that's its contradiction: the motions, graceful, natural, and uncomplicated, yet impossibly intricate, subtle, refined only after hundreds, thousands of attempts, throw and swing and catch and run—all in unison, a dance of spring. Baseball is reflexive even after forty years. The motions are indelible and welcomed, routine, something that can be counted on, like a Saturday morning, like an old friend.

This time, the ball shoots hard just to the left of second base, but Ben again is ready. He leaps across the base, snags the ball on one bounce, pivots, steps back, kicks the bag with a toe, and fires to Keith, who catches the ball at his chin.

"Yeah! Double play!" Keith hollers.

"We got him by two steps!" Ben says of the imaginary runner.

"Way to go, team, way to hustle," I say.

Next, I send Ben out to center field to shag flies. Keith takes a place beside me at home plate to retrieve Ben's throws as he sends the balls back. I toss up a ball and connect, punching it to Ben's left. He drifts under it.

"Two hands, Ben," I call out. "Use two hands."

As Ben throws it in, I toss up another ball, trying to hit it to Ben's right. But I miss and the ball lands at my feet.

"Damn, it's been a while since I swung a bat," I say to Keith. "My shoulder's killing me."

I try again, eye on the ball, this time sending a line drive to center. Ben gloves it handily on one bounce and flips it back into the infield.

"Ben seems to have gotten better since last year," I say to Keith. "But I don't know how that's possible, for all the sitting around he's done over the winter."

"Testosterone," Keith answers, and he's probably right.

Ben has grown and developed, lost his junior-high clumsiness. He's starting to grow into his body. He's more coordinated, nimble, moving comfortably without floundering about. His voice is changing, too, alternating in pitch and in force, one minute a dog whistle and the next a tuba.

I swat another dozen fly balls and then call Ben in for batting practice. My shoulder is throbbing, but I walk out to the mound with three baseballs in my glove to pitch. Keith plays shortstop.

"Take a few swings, Ben, swing evenly, don't try to kill it."

I hold the ball in my right hand, two fingers over the seams, and throw toward the plate. The ball sails behind Ben's head, missing him by inches and forcing him to duck.

"Hey! Geez, watch it, you trying to kill me?" he complains.

Keith lets out a big laugh.

"Okay, okay, let me move closer," I say, and I step up ten feet. I throw the next ball over the plate, but this time over Ben's head by five feet.

"All right, this one's coming over," I promise.

I lob the next ball in, a big lob, and Ben smacks it back to the mound, straight at me. I knock it down with my glove and stumble, nearly falling off my feet.

"We're even," I scowl, regaining my balance, and Ben gathers the other baseballs, chuckling to himself.

"I'm getting a little lonesome out here, guys," Keith says as Ben steps up to the plate again. "Hey, batter, come on, batter batter."

I throw another pitch and Ben connects again, a slow grounder to Keith. Keith runs up on the ball, bends, and scoops it out of the dirt. But it drops out of his glove, and he runs headlong onto the infield grass, trying to slow his legs.

"Next one, Ozzie, you'll get the next one," I heckle.

Ben returns to the batter's box, crouching, waiting. "Come on, pitcher," he says, "put it in here, let me hit it."

I kick the dust from an invisible pitching rubber, bend low, and look down behind the plate to an invisible catcher for the sign. I shake off the first sign, then nod my head. *Yes, I'll go with the fastball.* I swing my arms back, up, kick my left foot, twist, pull back my right arm, hurl forward, and release. It's a perfect strike, right down the gutter.

Ben swings, his full weight behind his bat, and meets the ball solidly, completely, a line drive, whistling through the air, up the middle of the infield. As he breaks into a run, Keith breaks to his left. He raises his glove across his chest to his shoulder, waits for the exact instant, and dives into the air. His glove opens, closes, and the little white ball disappears into leather.

"You're out!" I roar, and Ben stops dead at second base. He drops his hands to his knees and just stares.

Keith lies in the dirt on his back, spread-eagled, puffing, and he throws his glove over his head.

"Not bad for a couple of geezers," Ben says, shuffling back to the plate.

"Not bad at all," I say, and I walk over to Keith to give him a hand getting up.

I pull my car into the driveway late in the afternoon a week and a half later, and I notice Ben approaching on the sidewalk, coming home from school. His baseball shoes are laced together and slung over a shoulder, and in his right hand he holds his mitt with a slip of paper clenched in the pocket. Under his arm are a pair of white pants with red stripes down the legs and a white-and-red jersey. A baseball uniform.

"I made the team," he tells me as I open my car door.

"Hey, well, that makes my day," I cheer.

He bobs his head and shrugs, trying to take it in stride, trying not to make it into a big deal. But it is.

"How's this?"

Cathy files into a row of chairs in the high school cafeteria, and I follow behind her, Emma's hand in mine. We've come to Ben's school on this fine evening in early June to attend a student recognition ceremony. Ben is receiving an achievement award from the school's chapter of Quill and Scroll, an international honorary society that supports the staffs of school newspapers and yearbooks. He has worked as a reporter for the *Cardinal News* for the past year, and tonight is his night to shine.

Cathy, Emma, and I are the first family to arrive, just a bit early, I guess. It's a habit of mine, a virtue, in my opinion, a vice, in Cathy's.

"We're twenty minutes early," she says, leaning forward in her chair to capture my full attention, but I don't mind. We've got choice seats, the second row in a dozen. There are plenty of open chairs in the front row, but we dare not sit in the very front row. Ben is still uneasy about having his parents at his school. It's a personal-space issue, I suspect, and an identity thing. He's still uncomfortable separating his Ben-in-the-company-of-friends-and-teachers persona from his Ben-in-the-company-of-Mom-and-Dad persona. Sometimes these two Bens can be very different creatures. His laugh can be more boisterous when he's around his buddies, his walk more of a lumber. When he's with his family, he's still the same sweet kid he always was.

The school year is winding down; just three days remain. Wauwatosa East is a whirlwind of activity tonight. Beyond the glass walls of the cafeteria, in the school commons, cheerleaders are practicing, waving red and white pompoms over their heads and swirling with team spirit, while in the gymnasium an awards ceremony is being held for the basketball players. If forced to pigeon-hole the group of kids here in the cafeteria, I would call them bookworms, brainy kids, kids that I once termed goody-goodies, some of them on the nerdy side, fast readers, skillful writers, articulate speakers, poised, polite, clever—the type of kid I never was.

All around us now, mothers and fathers wander in and take their seats. Some of them are older than Cathy and I, some younger, some about the same age. There is no uniformity. We are neither old nor young, which comforts me somehow. I shift in my metal folding chair, waiting, watching.

Ben sits with his newspaper colleagues, trying to appear solemn under the glossy gaze of the family audience. He's wearing a white dress shirt, open at the collar, no tie, a gray tweed jacket, green chinos. Except for the big, black boots on his feet, he probably looks too much like his father. So, to spare him further from this embarrassment, I dressed this evening in a brown tweed jacket over a button-down denim shirt. The distinction, though, is lost on Cathy. "You two are doubles," she told us before we left the house. She wagged her head in disapproval but knew nothing could be done. We're father and son, with a limited wardrobe and an equally limited fashion sense.

Emma sits next to me, studying the program notes for this evening's ceremony.

"I know what s-c-h-o-o-l spells. *School*. What about this word, what does h-i-g-h spell?"

"It spells *high*," I say. "High and school, high school. *High* is a hard word to sound out, though, isn't it?"

Emma has experienced a burst of intellectual growth herself over the past few months. She's learning to read, and every waking moment leads to a lesson. She questions us constantly about words, sounding out titles on magazine covers, reading the backs of cereal boxes during breakfast. As she learns to read, her speech becomes more fluent, her stories more descriptive. She can go on with a story about her day at school for five minutes without taking a breath. As the year ends, I'm going to miss our daily eight o'clock walks to Washington School. It's been a special time for the two of us, a time to begin our days together.

Cathy, meanwhile, has completed her semester in college. She has tallied another year toward completing a degree in elementary ed and will continue classes through the summer, anxiously racing toward a new profession, with me right behind, cheering her on toward the finish line—and the work force.

The awards ceremony gets underway. Long candles are passed out to the new members of the Quill and Scroll society, who stand before the families in sort of a chorus line. As a freshman, Ben is not eligible for formal induction, so he sits to the side and observes as his cohorts are initiated. One by one, the students light candles and recite short pledges. The faculty advisor, Mrs. Barrington, then says a few kind words about each student's contribution, deftly emphasizing one or two commendable traits.

Lastly, Mrs. Barrington asks Ben to stand. He rises, shuffling his big boots awkwardly on the floor. He gives her a shy, crooked grin and folds his hands at his waist.

"Ben has worked tirelessly through the year as a new member of the staff, and the only freshman," Mrs. Barrington says. Ben scratches his jaw nervously. "He has gained a reputation for tackling the tough issues. His writing also has vastly improved over the course of the year and we look forward to having Ben as an editor next fall. Please congratulate him for an excellent job."

As the audience applauds, water fills my eyes and I must look down at the floor for a minute.

The ceremony ends and families are invited to help themselves to refreshments in the back of the room. Emma heads for the stack of sugar cookies, and Ben hangs back with his friends for a minute, basking in the glory, before joining his family.

"Can I have a cookie, Emma?" he says, and his sister obliges, handing Ben the one broken cookie out of the four in her hands.

"I'm proud of you," Cathy says, and she gives him a hug—a public hug, though, brief and restrained.

"Congratulations, Ben," I say, and I shake his hand. It's the manly thing to do, I think to myself, a handshake, a father's salute to his maturing son.

Ben is pleased with himself; I can see the satisfaction shine through. He's grateful to be recognized, glad to have found acceptance into this rather exclusive club, to have found a place in this fickle community called high school.

I think back to last fall when he began his freshman year, to how apprehensive he was then about high school. So much ancient history, now. He has done all right for himself. His teachers have heaped on the praise. He has made many close friends, friends who call him on weeknights for help with their homework, who seek him out each and every weekend for fun. Ben is self-aware, observant, thoughtful, blossoming into a true leader.

I try to tell him some of this, but the words just don't make it out of my heart.

"Congratulations, Ben," is all I can say.

Graceland

The back screen door opens, and Ben walks onto the patio. "What are you doing, Dad?"

"Right now, I'm restringing my guitar while drinking a tall glass of iced tea. Takes a lot of dexterity to do both, I must say."

I sit on the bench of our backyard picnic table, the acoustic guitar balanced across my knees. Ben takes a seat in a lawn chair across from me. The late afternoon sun casts long shadows across the cement patio. The smell of fresh-cut grass drifts up from the lawn, a springtime perfume.

"So how was your last day of school? You left the house so early this morning. How did everything go?"

"I got an A-minus on my science test."

"All right, terrific." I feed an E-string through a tuning peg. "And how about math?"

"I think I did okay on the final. I met with my math teacher this morning before school to study. I should get a B in precalculus. My only B."

"Hey, a B in precalculus is good work, don't knock it. You were so worried you'd only get a C in that class." The E-string sings higher and higher as I wind it tighter and tighter.

"So how does it feel to be free for the summer?" I ask him, "and a sophomore now?"

"I think I've got a job lined up already. A friend of mine said the country club is hiring caddies. He works there and said he might be able to get me in. I'm going to fill out an application tomorrow."

I wind the last of the six strings tight on the guitar, and I begin to tune. "What do they pay?"

"Probably minimum wage. Plus tips. And they let caddies golf for free on Mondays."

"Not a bad perk," I say. "When I was fifteen, I had a job as a busboy, clearing tables at DeeJay's restaurant. The pay wasn't much, but after closing, the busboys and the waitresses got a free dinner. Steak, lobster. Old Sal the chef cooked us anything we wanted."

"I don't think I'd want to work in a restaurant, not unless I could cook," he says. "I'd rather work outside."

I start strumming the guitar softly as we talk. "The worst job I ever had was working as a butcher's assistant in a grocery store," I say. "Man. It was terrible. I cut meat and ground up hamburger all day. I didn't last long."

Ben picks up a tennis ball lying on the cement. He throws it into the air and catches it with one hand.

"It's going to be a busy summer," I say. "You might be working. Emma's going to day camp. Cathy's going to summer school. I'll be teaching."

"Teaching where?"

"I'm teaching a writing class through the university. Just one course. I'm looking forward to it. I've also got a huge writing assignment due soon, and I've just sent out a batch of résumés. I'm going to look for a full-time job on a magazine staff. This freelance life just isn't cutting it."

He bounces the tennis ball between his shoes and asks a question. "Are we going to take a road trip this year, you and me? Last year's trip was great."

A year ago, leaving on Father's Day, the two of us set out for Washington, D.C., and the Appalachian Mountains. We were on the road for nearly two weeks. I had no schedule to keep, one of the few benefits of my hit-or-miss occupation as a freelance writer. We toured the national monuments in Washington, explored the museums, hiked a stretch of the Appalachian Trail, camped along the seashore, and spent a day at Jefferson's Monticello. We both had a great time.

"I haven't really thought about it."

"I think we should," he says, determinedly. And then he says something that catches me off guard, something I'd heard myself say before, something I said when I quit my full-time job two years ago and set out for new horizons. "Just remember, Dad: Don't confuse your job with your life."

Ben was giving me advice, my own advice, and good advice at that. It helps to be reminded of your own ideals.

"Maybe you're right, Ben, maybe you're right."

Ben tosses the tennis ball onto the roof of the garage and catches it as it bounces to the patio. He looks across the patio to the driveway. "Where's your car?"

"I gave it away," I answer. "Gave it to a nonprofit camp for troubled kids. They repair old cars and resell them or sell the parts to raise money."

"It's gone?"

"The old Subaru is gone, yes. It was brought back from the dead one too many times. It was just too dangerous to drive, a bucket of bolts, 'a clinking, clanking, clattering collection of caliginous junk,' in the words of the Wizard. The brakes were almost gone. I had to keep the window open all the time. Fumes from a cracked exhaust pipe were seeping in through a hole in the floor. That's not good."

I take a swallow of iced tea. "Lot of memories in that car, though," I add. "We drove to the East Coast when Cathy was pregnant with Emma. *That* was a mistake. We had to stop every six or seven miles for her to use a bathroom. She was not in a very adventurous mood on that vacation."

"I remember that," says Ben. "We stayed in Boston with Aunt Julie and Uncle Steve and my cousin Bari. We went to Fenway for a game."

"That's right. Boston played the Tigers, I think. We sat along the third-base line, good seats. Cecil Cooper hit a home run over the Green Monster."

"Grandma Shirlee flew up from Florida when we were there, and we all drove to Maine, stayed at bed-and-breakfasts along the ocean. That was a great trip."

"You weren't the one who was pregnant," I answer, finger-picking the guitar frets, making up a melody. "We drove that car out West on another vacation when you were younger, maybe six. To the Black Hills, Mount Rushmore, all the way down to Mesa Verde in southwest Colorado. Remember those Indian ruins, the Anasazi cliff dwellings? We had to climb a ladder to get from level to level? Amazing place. That little Subaru was a tour bus, a taxi, an ambulance. Breakneck drives to the maternity ward, forgotten lunches delivered to your school. All that chauffeuring to Cub Scouts, Boy Scouts, Little League, the library. All the trips between Minneapolis and Milwaukee."

"So what are you going to do for a car?"

"I'm going to buy a friend's old Volvo next week. We'll be a two-Volvo family."

"Not another Volvo! Why don't you get something smaller, something *sportier*?"

Ben has a sudden stake in the cars we own. He'll be learning to drive late in the summer. With his learner's permit in his back pocket, he will soon be sliding behind the wheel of an automobile. Behind the wheel of a Volvo. After he completes the classroom instruction and behind-the-wheel training, I will become his teacher, showing him how to pass on two-lane country highways, leading him through double-left-hand-lane turns, guiding him through rush-hour traffic and down one-way streets. I'm not worried, but I'm not ready yet, either, and I don't think Ben is. If I had my druthers, he would not drive until he was eighteen, or older. Automobiles are deadly weapons. The fatality rate for car crashes is highest for sixteen-year-old males. But peer pressure is a mighty force. Ben already has marked the date on his calendar when he'll be eligible for his temps.

"Volvos," I say to him, "are the safest cars on the road."

"Volvos are *boring*, they're so stodgy and square."

"I'm square too, Ben."

I rest my guitar on the picnic table and join him in his game of catch. He throws the tennis ball onto the roof and I catch it in my left hand before it hits the ground.

"It's time to par-*ty!*" Ben says into the telephone later that day. School is over, and Ben and his freshman buddies are ready to break loose.

I volunteer to drive him and three of his friends to a party. They gather at our home and pile into the back seat of the Volvo, Cathy's Volvo.

On the way, an overheated boy in the back seat gets a bit out of control. "This car smells like leather," he says loudly. "It smells like Lisa!"

The party is close by, a half-mile away. I pull up to the house and stop at the curb. Through the living room window, I see a crowd of teenagers standing and talking, moving their arms in animated gestures.

"Thanks a lot, Dad," says Ben. "We'll get a ride home from Chris's dad."

As they open the back door, the overheated kid goes over the top: "Let's bite everyone at the party!" he proposes, and they hop out of the car, yowling and yelping in the night.

I shake my head. It's our own damn fault, I say to no one. This is what my permissive generation has wrought.

* * *

Sunrise on a Saturday, the day before Father's Day, and Ben and I are up with the birds, but making a much less joyful sound.

"Wrz mah shha?" he grumbles, as he stands in his dim bedroom, his eyes just two slits above a nose.

"What?" I ask, not quite able to make the translation.

"Red sneaker. Can't find it."

Morning conversation with a teenager is a warm-up exercise. It begins as a series of low, muffled grunts and gradually builds into short words, then fragmented sentences, and finally something that resembles broken English, but heavy with attitude. I've learned not to rush the process. Though I've become more of a morning person the older I get, there is no point in trying to compel a fifteen-year-old boy to appreciate the beauty of a spring dawn. It would be easier to have him tested for rabies.

The two of us have a purpose for waking at 5:15 A.M.: We are hitting the road for this Father's Day weekend. To round out the year, with Ben's freshman experience now under his belt, we have rented a car and charted a course due south—to Memphis, Tennessee. To Graceland.

As I have known since my own teenage days, the road lends itself to exploration. We will leave behind Ben's mother and sister, pick a highway, and drive, see what we can learn about the places we visit, about life, and about each other. This is our tradition now, every Father's Day, hitting the road together.

Last year's trip to the East Coast went a long way toward strengthening our father–son bond, a relationship that's always in need of attention, always changing, and, one hopes, always growing stronger. This year Graceland will be our celebration, a celebration of the year.

In the morning light, I inspect a small pile of personal belongings on the dining room table: a stack of cassette tapes, a pack of Juicy Fruit, a yo-yo, a Swiss Army knife, athlete's foot cream, a red baseball cap, a polished stone in the shape of Wisconsin, and a book, *The Authoritative Calvin and Hobbes.*

"Don't forget your toothbrush," I call in a whisper.

Ben shuffles, both red sneakers now on his feet, from his bedroom to the bathroom to brush his teeth.

"Wihhn bwee ghlbbng?" he asks, talking through the Colgate.

"We'll leave in about ten minutes," I answer, quite sure I've deciphered his question. "We'll drive for an hour or so and stop for breakfast."

I open our atlas and flatten it on the kitchen table. Neither of us has been to Memphis. The home of the King seems like a good target.

"Look," I say, drawing an invisible line southward on a map of the United States. "It's a straight drop to Memphis, less than a day's drive. We'll get a motel tonight and tour Graceland tomorrow. I called to make reservations. We're booked for the Platinum Tour."

"Woo*hoo*," Ben says, a trace of sarcasm in his voice. Elvis is no idol of his, nor of mine, though I have my favorite Elvis hits. As many times as I've heard it, "All Shook Up" still sets my voice to a tremolo and invites me to s-s-s-sing along.

"Graceland is more than a monument to a dead rock 'n' roll star," I say. "Graceland is a slice of Americana, unique. We've gotta see it."

Graceland has become almost mythical. It's a curiosity that will be satisfied in a way that we do not yet know.

Ben agrees to leave behind his Walkman, a noble sacrifice. He seems to have that thing on his head all the time lately—in the car, at the computer screen at home, as he walks out the front door on his way to school.

"Maybe we can actually talk as we drive," I say to him.

"Don't push it, Dad," he says, his first complete sentence of the day.

The choice of music for the trip is a different matter.

"So what tapes are you bringing?" I ask, inspecting Ben's stack of cassettes. I read the labels out loud: "Crash Test Dummies,

Rage Against the Machine, Counting Crows, REM. Sponge. Wait a minute. I can't handle Sponge. Too much headbanger stuff."

"What do you mean?" he says. "I like 'em."

"I can't listen to 'em. Especially in the car."

"Well, what about *your* tapes?" And he circles the table to check the cassettes that I've selected. "Paul Simon, Neil Young, *Willie Nelson*?" He wrinkles his face. "No way, Dad. *Anything* but Willie Nelson."

"What? Willie Nelson is quintessential road music," I argue. "What are you talking about?"

"I can't take his voice. And besides, it's *country* music."

"Country, it's more than country," I try to explain. "It's Willie."

"If you get Willie, I get Sponge."

"Okay, okay, a compromise: Each of us gets veto power. Like lawyers in a trial during jury selection. Each of us can veto, what, two tapes?"

He thinks about this for a second, then agrees.

"So I veto Sponge," I say. "And this one, Rage Against the Machine."

"All right, no Willie Nelson," he returns. "And no Mary Chapin Carpenter. More *country*," he scoffs.

"Deal."

We start loading the car. We're traveling light: a suitcase, a couple of sport jackets, a camera bag, a small cooler. We stock the front seat with a plastic bottle of water, a roll of quarters for the tollways, and an economy-size bag of pretzels.

Cathy stands in the kitchen, two hands around a coffee mug, a smile on her lips as she watches us stumble to finish our packing. Emma sleeps soundly upstairs.

"We'll call you tonight," I say, feeling a twinge of guilt for leaving Emma and Cathy behind.

"Just have fun," she says, fluffing her sleepy brown curls with her fingers. "This is a trip Ben will always remember, and so will you. And someday you and Emma can go off somewhere together. Maybe Graceland, who knows?"

Ben hoists his backpack over his shoulder. He kisses his mother goodbye.

"Have a great time," she says.

I give her a hug and a kiss, tell her to give Emma a big kiss for her daddy and brother, then follow Ben out the screen door. The eastern sky has turned watercolor orange. Our rented Chevy Monte Carlo sits in the driveway, gleaming black, ready and waiting. We are on our way.

Speeding down the interstate, halfway to Chicago from our Milwaukee home, already there is a sense of consequence about our journey together. I'm energized, buoyant.

"There's nothing like a road trip," I say, glancing at Ben as I settle behind the wheel for the long drive. Feeling the even motion of the vehicle, eyes stretched to the horizon, attentive to everything beyond the glass, on the edge, never knowing what to expect—I'm giddy with anticipation, my left foot tapping on the floorboard. Anything is possible, I tell myself.

Ben studies the map, his baseball cap shielding his eyes from the sun.

"We got a good jump on the day," I say, trying to draw him into the motion, into the sensation. "Not much traffic so far."

He yawns. "The atlas says it's 622 miles to Memphis from Milwaukee," he says, slowly coming to life.

"That's nothing. What, maybe ten hours? We'll be there for dinner, no problem." We roll across the Illinois state line, silver dew sparkling on green farm fields.

I pull off the road for breakfast, as I had promised. The restaurant is a "travel oasis" north of Chicago, a steel-and-glass structure that spans all six lanes of Interstate 94. This place has been a wonder to me since I was a boy. Every six months, my parents would drive to Illinois to buy a case of oleomargarine. By law, colored *oleo*, as it was known then, could not be bought or sold in the dairy state of Wisconsin, a protectionist measure to promote the sale of butter. But to save a little money, my father bought oleo. On our runs across the border, he never failed to stop at the oasis.

Car trips and Sunday drives were regular events for my family. When I was about ten, we owned a 1960 Mercury four-door sedan, cream-colored. In order to hold four kids and two adults in that car, my father built a temporary bed that fit behind the front seat over the drive-shaft hump. My mother padded the plywood frame with blankets and pillows, and we kids would stretch out—three on the expanded back seat and one in the back window, the choice spot. Not the safest ride, of course; no one wore seat belts in those days. But it was a practical way of containing four road-silly children for a day in the car. The better option would have been a station wagon. But my father stubbornly refused to own one.

"I drive my panel truck around all day long, to and from the job sites," he said. "I don't want a station wagon. I want a nice, comfortable sedan."

That Mercury eventually began to rust, and the chassis began to sit crooked on the frame. As it worsened, the car rode sideways down the street, cockeyed by maybe twenty degrees to the right, noticeable enough that people would do double takes as we drove by. My mother was humiliated driving that car to church every Sunday, and she finally insisted that my father replace it. He bought another Mercury, a newer model but used, as always. And once again, he refused to buy a station wagon.

"This place is kind of cool," says Ben as we walk into the oasis.

"Used to be much cooler," I say. Once it was a Leave-It-to-Beaver, burger-and-malt diner, chrome stools at the counter, vinyl booths along the windows. Now it's a Burger King, all yellow and orange, plastic-coated for our convenience, disinfected for our protection. But it's still an uncommon attraction—a restaurant over the freeway.

We order our fast-food meals and sit by the window, watching the endless traffic below as it moves south: a limousine, a motorcycle, semi-trailers, camping trailers, minivans, pickups, sports cars, jeeps, convertibles . . .

"Where the heck are they all going?" I wonder out loud as we eat. Ten minutes later, we join the flow.

To kill time, we tune the radio to Chicago news broadcasts, feeling strangely removed from the controversies and crises of the day as we glide along the hot asphalt. Or we just gaze silently at the landscape as the odometer dutifully records our progress. The sky turns overcast white, the air heavy with Midwestern humidity. The countryside is the same everywhere we look: farmland, flat and fertile, green fields flying by on both sides of the black ribbon of road. Occasionally, a development of identical houses springs out of the fields for no apparent reason, an instant community borne of the latest boomtown. But the view from behind the windshield is mostly Illinois flatland, unobstructed, good for stretching the eyes, good for allowing thoughts to run.

The silence between us is comfortable. When driving alone sometimes with my father, even on short trips, the gaps between conversation felt strained and everlasting. He was busy in his own world and seldom willing to let me join him. I counted the telephone poles outside my window as we drove along.

"Dad, I think you took the wrong turn back there," Ben says suddenly, looking up from the map.

"Huh? Are you sure?"

"You were supposed to stay on I-57 south. We're on 55. We're heading to St. Louis."

My sense of direction usually is pretty good. But after looking at the atlas, I see that Ben is right.

"I must have spaced out."

"Duh," he chides. "You can get back on track just after Bloomington. Take I-74 east to Urbana."

Ben sits with the atlas opened on his lap for most of the day, double-checking my navigation now, alerting me to the next big junction, measuring our pace, telling me how far it is to Champaign, to Effingham, to Cairo. He's a good copilot, feeding music to the tape player—"I could go for some Willie Nelson," I lament—and keeping us supplied with bottles of juice or lemonade from the cooler in the back seat.

We stop for gas, and as a little diversion, we decide to time our pit stop. I reel to a halt at the Amoco gas pumps and the clock starts ticking. I fill the gas tank as Ben stocks up on Snickers and potato chips. I fling a twenty-dollar bill at the cashier and Ben and I race to the men's room and back to the Monte Carlo. We're on the road again in seven minutes flat, hooting and hollering as we pull behind the same convoy of pink Cadillacs (piloted by Mary Kay Cosmetics reps, dolled-up and ready to peddle their brushed-on beauty) that we'd passed twenty miles back.

I merge onto I-74 east, as per Ben's instructions, and we're back on track. The weather is clear, the road is straight, and the miles just sail by. The drive is effortless. But maybe too effortless: In southern Illinois, just five minutes from the Mississippi River and the Missouri border, I get nailed in a speed trap. I notice a dark car parked conspicuously on an overpass as I hurry along, and sure enough, a quarter-mile later, a state patrolman flags me down from the side of the interstate.

"Damn," I say, as I pull over to the shoulder. "I thought I could make up some lost time for that wrong turn back there." I roll down my window as the patrolman appears, a character right out of a Hitchcock movie. Dark sunglasses, a thin, foreboding smile, round hat topping a dark brown uniform.

"Good afternoon, sir," he says with a slightly Southern accent, not removing his shades. "You were clocked doing eighty-five miles per hour in a sixty-five miles per hour speed zone." And then he asks the unanswerable: "Do have a reason for driving that fast, sir?"

I have no reason at all, not even a good lie. I mumble something about not realizing my speed, about the beautiful spring day, but my words are futile.

"Can I see your license, please?" He takes it and steps back to his patrol car.

"What do you think he'll do?" Ben asks.

"I think I'm doomed."

"You just got a ticket a couple of weeks ago, didn't you?"

"For an illegal U-turn. Thanks for reminding me."

Five minutes later, the officer returns.

"Sir, I'm going to issue you a summons for speeding. If I write you up at eighty-five miles per hour, you will be required to appear in court in person. But I'm only going to cite you for doing eighty-four. That way, you can mail in your fine. I believe it's seventy-five dollars. Consider this a favor, sir. Consider this your lucky day."

I nod, smile, take the ticket, and thank the officer. Ingrained Catholic guilt, I suppose.

"Lucky day," I repeat to Ben, and I swing the big black Chevy back into traffic. "Maybe I'll win the lottery next."

"I suppose it could've been worse," Ben says. "He *could* have made you go to court. Then we would've been kind of screwed."

But I won't be appeased. I leave Illinois in a huff, pissed off at my fate.

We cross the Big Muddy, arching high on a bridge. Barges inch along far below, and I imagine Huck and Tom paddling their raft in the shade of the wooded banks. My aggravation is gone by the time we touch down into Missouri. We ride the Missouri interstate for just a short stretch, cutting along the western loops of the Mississippi at precisely the legal speed, then scoot into Arkansas for a few miles, parallel to the river. The Chevrolet is humming with expectation.

"Yessss! I can add Arkansas to my list," Ben says, counting to himself. "Tennessee will make thirty-six states total."

"You're catching up to me," I say. "Let's see. I'll be at forty-five. Tennessee will make forty-five states. I'm still missing Mississippi, both Carolinas, and I've got to get to Hawaii and Alaska."

Half an hour later, we cross the zigzagging Mississippi River again and roll into Memphis. We exit the freeway, finally, and follow Crump Boulevard along the south side of town. It's five o'clock. The Memphis afternoon is hot, delta steamy, even late in the day. Our air conditioner in the car has been set on high, with the windows rolled up tight. But when we get to Memphis, I roll down my window and stick out my arm. I want to hear Memphis, to smell Memphis, to feel it, to sweat in the soggy heat of this river town.

"Let's drive downtown," I say, "down to Beale Street. Get us to Beale Street, Ben." He finds a map of Memphis and quickly orients us.

"Okay, turn left on Third Street," Ben says. He squints through the windshield as we come to the next intersection. "Yeah, that should take us downtown."

I follow his directions and, before long, we're heading for the glass high-rise buildings of the downtown business district. The city streets are busy with cars, the sidewalks thick with pedestrians as Saturday afternoon turns to Saturday evening.

"This should be Beale Street coming up," Ben says as we stop for a red light.

A stream of people pours across the crosswalk. Old Beale Street, the home of the blues, is jumping. At each end, the street is barricaded, blocked off to cars, and folks are milling about down the center line, drinks in their hands, drifting in and out of gift shops and restaurants and clubs, music pouring from open doors and windows.

"This is where we want to be," I say, and I cue the Paul Simon song that I've been saving for this very minute. I roll down all of the windows and turn the volume way up. And, as we pull away

from the stoplight, at the top of our lungs, like the tourists that we are, for all of Memphis to hear, we announce our arrival in song:
I'm going to Graceland, Graceland.
Memphis, Tennessee . . .

Ben laughs at our foolishness, embarrassed, I can tell, yet he sings anyway, and I see that it is my lucky day after all. It has been a big year for Ben, for both of us, a year worth singing about. With my hero in the passenger seat and the sun sinking down, all is right with the world. We're explorers in a new city, filled with wonder and anticipation.

We both will be received in Graceland.

Later that night we find a restaurant on Beale Street for dinner. It's nothing fancy, a barbecue joint with a horseshoe-shaped bar and a dozen tables, but it's packed with people, tourists and locals, here for the ribs. We wait in line outside for fifteen minutes before we're finally led in. We sit at a round wooden table next to the front window, looking out onto the street. The place is noisy, and smoky from cigarettes; the service is slow, the waitresses moving as fast as they can in the packed room. We don't mind. We're in no hurry. We have no schedule. Just Graceland tomorrow, the 11 A.M. Platinum Tour.

"What are you going to order?" Ben asks as we scan the menu.

"I'm thinking about the catfish," I say. "Catfish dinner with red beans and rice and a beer."

"That's sounds good to me. Without the beer."

"Memphis is bigger than I thought," I say, looking out the window. "A river town, reminds me a little of the Twin Cities, St. Paul along the river."

"I'd like to get a T-shirt."

"Maybe an Elvis shirt?"

"No, not Elvis. Something more tasteful."

"I don't know if you're going to find tasteful," I answer. "I have a feeling the souvenir shops around Graceland trade in things tacky. My friend Paul asked me to buy him an Elvis Pez dispenser, if I can find one."

"Now that's tacky."

The waitress arrives to take our order, a young woman with a sweet smile, her blonde hair tied back. Ben orders first.

"I'd like the catfish dinner, um, and beans, the red beans, I guess. And rice. Red beans and rice. And, do you have, like, ginger ale?"

I look at Ben across the table. Plain white T-shirt, red baseball cap still on his head, the fuzzy outline of sideburns forming on his smooth skin. I listen to him place his order, slightly self-conscious. I watch him glance at the young waitress, though only for a split second, watch him fumble with his fork, fold the corner of his placemat, unsure what to do with his hands, watch him lift the cloth napkin and lay it on his lap, watch him wipe his hair out of his face and eye the people in the crowd, watch him ponder the world, watch his boyish jaw form his conversation. His moods can swing by the minute, from giggly and goofy to get-out-of-my-face indifferent. He's still trapped by that awkward, herky-jerky motion of a boy's body. Yet on this marvelous June evening, Ben straddles the line between childhood and adolescence. When he talks, his words are serious, considered, his voice dropping now to the lower registers. When he walks, his stride is just a half-step short of a man's.

Soon his awkwardness will leave him and his voice will find a home and his bones will harden and he will take his place on the other side of childhood.

After a long wait, our dinner is served. We're hungry now at nearly nine o'clock.

"Good beans and rice," Ben declares, shoveling them in.

Waitresses dash back and forth, working overtime for their tips. On a stage at the back of the restaurant, a band is tuning up, a three-piece group, bass, guitar, drums.

"It looks like we're going to hear some music," I say.

The musicians smile at the crowd and start into an up-tempo song, three-chord stomping Memphis blues. People look up from their food and drinks and start moving in rhythm to the bass drum. Ben bobs his head side to side like one of those dolls in the back window of a car, off the beat a bit but energetic, drunk on the ginger ale and the bustle of the bar. I take a few big gulps of beer, emptying my glass, my reward for the long day of driving, the miles melting away with each gulp.

The band plays hard-driving blues, good-time music, enlivening the patrons and turning dinner time into party time. After a couple of songs, the guitar player introduces a singer, a black woman with big hair and a bigger frame. She steps onto the stage and the band launches into rhythm and blues. The singer's gold-sequined dress crawls up her thighs as she begins to dance, holding the microphone in one hand and beckoning to the crowd with the other, cocking her head and belting out the high notes. Her voice dips and rolls, soars and drops down to just a whisper, then breaks loose in a shout, shaking the liquor bottles on the back bar and pulling people to their feet, clapping and dancing, whooping and howling back at the singer. She struts along at the edge of the platform, swinging her queen-sized hips. The place is mobbed, people standing between tables. As her voice carries into the street, a throng gathers at the open front door, transfixed.

Ben watches, unblinking, examining the singer, the band, the crowd. He shouts something at me, but I can't hear him. I nod and wave, thinking I have an idea what he's said. He has never been to a club like this before, never heard such impulsive, lawless music, and he's digging it, digging the blues, on a Saturday night, on Beale Street, in Memphis, Tennessee.

The set ends, I pay the waitress, and Ben and I step outside. The street is flooded with people, a girl with a green ice-cream cone melting down her arm, a man and a woman in matching Elvis T-shirts walking a white poodle, a family of tap dancers performing to a circle of tourists, a juggler tossing fire into the sky from atop a unicycle. It's a circus, a holiday.

We walk down the centerline of Beale, taking it all in.

I've known nights like this before. You find yourself in a place foreign and strange, and suddenly circumstances tumble into position and lift you up with the force of a hurricane, big and blustery, unstoppable, a force that you did not expect. You might be on Beale Street in Memphis or a familiar street near your home in Milwaukee. It doesn't matter. Something clicks and you go along as the events unfold, curious and a little careless. You welcome the unexpected, tapping your foot, shaking your head, losing yourself in the moment, in the spontaneity, guileless and awakened to all possibilities. It's magical, a gift, a moment you won't forget. And you realize that the moment is like so much else in life: you can't plan for it or predict it, but you need to be open to it when it comes, ready to embrace it and join in. You must jump in with both feet or sit it out and grow old.

The Platinum package includes a tour of the mansion, the mansion grounds, the trophy hall, a museum housing Elvis's customized automobiles, and a back lot storing his customized planes. We begin with the mansion and the living quarters of Elvis, Priscilla, and their only child, Lisa Marie. We board a tour bus at Graceland headquarters and take a short drive across Elvis Presley Boulevard, through a set of iron gates and up to the front door.

The tour is self-guided. Each visitor is fitted with a portable cassette tape player on a shoulder strap and a pair of headphones. Put on the headphones, slip in a tape, step up to the front door, and Elvis welcomes you in song—*Love me tender, love me true*—followed by a prerecorded recitation on the mansion's history and decor.

Ben refuses to wear the headset. Though he lives in his Walkman at home, he won't be corrupted by a taped guided tour.

"I don't want to listen to a recording, that's bogus," he says. He wants to experience Graceland in a pure manner, with no electronic devices, no virtual enhancements, no artificial additives. Teenage principles.

"Suit yourself," I tell him as we stand in line in front of the house.

The mansion is antebellum style, built of flagstone. Granite lions greet guests on either side of the walkway. Tall, white pillars flank the entryway, creating a portico. Black shutters border the windows, each window covered by a metal security grate.

We walk through the front door. To the left is the dining room: a long table where Elvis and Priscilla held famous dinner parties, a china cabinet, knickknacks on a buffet—a fairly typical dining room, really.

Across from the dining room is the living room, with an ivory sofa, two matching chairs, a blond wood coffee table, and floor-to-ceiling mirrors in the corners. Theater ropes keep visitors out, but we can look into a room beyond, the music room, furnished with a gleaming black grand piano and a television set inside a huge wooden console. The room is dimly lit, and I can almost hear the King crooning "Crying in the Chapel" at the piano.

"This is kind of interesting," Ben says, "not as tacky as I thought it'd be."

"Well, we're not done yet."

Off the kitchen, we step into the famous Jungle Room, so named because of the motif of the decor—green shag carpet, a fountain built into a wall of rock, and a giant easy chair that resembles a tree stump, large enough to fit the latter-day Elvis. According to the taped tour guide, Elvis converted this room into a recording studio and made many of his last records here, filling the place with studio musicians and friends.

Next, we follow a narrow staircase downstairs to the Rumpus Room, Elvis's hideaway. The room is decorated in gold and black and equipped with a full bar, a jukebox, an elaborate sound

197

system, and an enormous collection of record albums. The ceiling is mirrored glass, and against one wall, three television sets are turned on. The tape says Elvis came down to his Rumpus Room to listen to music while watching TV, all three networks at once.

I remove my headphones. "Let's take a break," I say, and we walk outside to the backyard. A swing set stands near a stone walkway, unused. On a wide lawn at the back of the grounds, horses graze in the sun, penned behind a white fence.

I take a breath of air. "I feel like I'm in the 1977 Parade of Homes all of a sudden," I say. "I've lived in places with that same green shag carpet."

"For some reason I didn't expect so much stuff to be inside— the kitchen plates and all his records and that," Ben says. "It's all right. But I don't see the big attraction, really. It's just a house. And it's a lot smaller than I thought it'd be."

"The place looks like it was lived in, I'll say that."

The Home of the King, so fascinating and so meaningful to so many people. It says something about celebrity, about heroes in our country: how we hold in such high esteem the life of a singer dead now for more than twenty years, instead of the people who have the greatest influence on us, who can truly make a difference—our friends, parents, grandparents. Our children.

"This is the seventh time I've been to Graceland," gushes a woman to her friend as they rush past us. Ben and I look at each other, and he shrugs.

For Ben and me, it's not Elvis. It's not Graceland or any other tourist trap that's important. The place itself doesn't matter much. It's a point on a map, a destination, an adventure that we can say we've had. Just being here—it's a memory in the making, a story being written, the passing of time together, father and son.

We roam through the backyard, no tour guides to usher us along, no timetable to keep. At the back of the mansion is a small swimming pool, potted flowers, and a few deck chairs arranged on a stone-tile patio, nothing ostentatious in the least. The "medita-tion garden," though, is another story. The garden is a private family graveyard, lush, majestic. Entombed here in an elliptical plot of ground are Elvis; his father, Vernon; his mother, Gladys; and his grandmother, Minnie Mae. Huge bronze tablets cover each grave, inscribed with names, dates, and blessings. Fresh flowers adorn each site. A large circular fountain gushes in the garden's center, and overlooking the family tomb is a white mar-ble statue of Jesus, fifteen feet high, with two angels kneeling at his side.

The garden is crowded with visitors, curious pilgrims, people of all ages. Ben wanders about, circling the garden, reading the inscriptions on each of the tombs. I sit on a red brick step near the swimming pool and watch a father and his teenage daughter as they enter the meditation garden. The girl is about Ben's age, with long hair, blue-jean shorts, and a white T-shirt with a dol-phin on the front. It's hard to tell the father's age; it always is. He's wearing khakis, white running shoes, a Dallas Cowboys polo shirt. His hair is blond, thinning on top. A pair of smoky tinted glasses cover his eyes. They walk side by side, father and daughter, around the fountain, and stop at the tomb of Elvis. They crouch down together and touch the short iron fence in front of the tomb. They stare at the grave and they stand. The father steps back, slides his glasses up onto his head, lifts a camera to his eye, and points it at his daughter. He waves her in closer and snaps a picture. Then he turns, looks around, and spots me sitting on the step nearby.

"Would you do the honors?" he asks.

"Of course," I say. He hands me the camera and puts his arm around his daughter's shoulder, smiling, proud, and sincere, but looking a bit self-conscious too, posing at the grave of Elvis.

Fathers do their best. We each follow our father's steps and we each make our own. My father did his best. Having never known his father, he had no one to follow, little to go on. His methods were his alone, right and wrong, good and bad. I hope to improve on the role—it is the duty of all fathers—correcting when I can, bettering, gaining, refining, building on what I saw as good, throwing out what I think was wrong, enriching and expanding the experiences of fatherhood in a way that my father would not or could not.

Some experiences are born of the times, following the trends of a generation or evolving with the latest technology. My father helped me restore an old bicycle; I taught my son how to ride a dirt bike in the north woods. My father showed me how to build a bridge over the backyard creek; I helped Ben write a newspaper story on the computer.

Other experiences arise as each father becomes his own man, each with different values and different ideals. Fishing for walleye in a Wisconsin lake with my father became snorkeling among the barracuda in the Florida Keys with Ben. Watching war movies on TV in the living room became sitting in the bleachers at a rock concert.

And some things stay the same, sturdy, constant, emblematic of this ever-demanding but profoundly rewarding practice known as fatherhood: a game of catch, the chauffeured drive of a son's first date, a shaving lesson.

If Ben becomes a father one day—and I hope he does—he will make his own choices, follow his own path, rejecting some of my methods and manners, I am sure, while shaping new ones and modifying others. Perhaps he will embrace some of my ideas, see some of my choices as consequential, even wise. I won't hold him to it. He will make his own way in the role. But perhaps he will have learned something from me over the years, and will carry on and *advance* what he's gained, in his own style yet as a father's tradition—if not a hike in the mountains on a rainy afternoon, then maybe an expedition to the top of Mount Everest; if not a road trip to Graceland, then maybe a trip to the stars.

* * *

Ben takes a seat beside me on the red brick steps, resting his elbows on his knees.

"Today's Father's Day, Dad," he says. "Happy Father's Day." He leans into me and knocks his forehead onto my shoulder a couple of times, gentle taps of affection.

"Yes it is, it sure is." I brush the hair from his right eye. "Thanks, Ben."

The sky is beginning to change colors. A wind bends the tree-tops in the backyard, and the horses dance across the velvet lawn.

"So what do you think about next year?" I ask. "Where should we go next? Cooperstown? The Grand Canyon? Maybe Alaska someday?"

"Yeah, Dad. Sure. All of them. Anywhere."

"You got it."

And I stand to ask a father if he will take our picture.

ACKNOWLEDGMENTS

This is a book made possible by family—immediate and extended, biological and otherwise. I am fondly grateful to my wife, Cathy, for her teeth-grinding, brow-furrowing patience, to my daughter, Emma, for her constant brightness, and to my son, Ben, for trusting my judgment without question, wisely or not.

I am thankful to my mother for her undampable spirit and bountiful memories; to my brothers, Steve and Greg, and my sister, Kathleen, for their steady support; to my mother-in-law, Shirlee Brun, for always finding the silver lining; to Linda Barrington, the exceptional teacher that she is, for guiding Ben along; to Judy Bridges at Redbird Writing Studios for her smiling words of encouragement; to John Fennell, my editor at *Milwaukee Magazine*, for letting me air out my aims and complaints; and to my good friend, Keith Prochnow, for suggesting this idea in the first place.

I also want to thank Jane Dystel, my agent, for her unflagging commitment, and Jay Schaefer, my editor at Chronicle Books, for his guidance in keeping me on the mark.

Finally, I want to commend all the dads I know who make the time for wholehearted fatherhood.